Letters in Vessels

Letters in Vessels
A Memoir

Anthony Diamandi

XULON ELITE

Xulon Press Elite
2301 Lucien Way #415
Maitland, FL 32751
407.339.4217
www.xulonpress.com

© 2019 by Anthony Diamandi

All rights reserved solely by the author. The author guarantees all contents are original and do not infringe upon the legal rights of any other person or work. No part of this book may be reproduced in any form without the permission of the author. The views expressed in this book are not necessarily those of the publisher.

Unless otherwise indicated, Scripture quotations taken from the New King James Version (NKJV). Copyright © 1982 by Thomas Nelson, Inc. Used by permission. All rights reserved.

Printed in the United States of America.

ISBN-13: 978-1-6305-0136-5

Table of Contents

1. First Letter. 1
2. Flickering to Burn 3
3. At the Main Street Pier 7
4. Something Supernatural. 9
5. Under the Main Street Pier. 11
6. A Song, Opened Eyes, and Miracles 15
7. A Closer Walk. 19
8. My Exodus 25
9. Boot Camp Letters. 31
10. Lincoln Letters 43
11. Held Up in Prayer 65
12. Japan Letters. 81
13. Two Become Three 89
14. Nimitz Letters. 101
15. I Live For You in Dedication to Her 121
16. In Closing 127

1

First Letter

Letter: a written, typed, or printed communication, especially one in an envelope by mail or messenger. ([1]Stevenson and Lindberg, Oxford American Dictionary, 1003.)

At the age of twenty-two, I had forgotten how to communicate with God. As a child, there was an extreme closeness to God, like I was in His hands. As a young man, I felt like I had walked so far away from His hands that I did not know how to get back. My life was in shambles with glimpses of light in the form of my girlfriend and family shining through the darkness. There was a strong urge inside of me to get my life back together for them. There was no way of doing it on my own. God was leading me back to Him gently. I forgot how to pray, so I came to Him through writing. I wrote my first letter to Him. It all started with this letter, and this was the beginning of our relationship.

First Letter (October 2001)

Dear God,
    This seems like the best way of communication for myself, writing that is. I know You know this. I would like to apologize for

Letters in Vessels

putting my prayers on paper. I know my head is down while I write to You, however, I will finish these prayers to You with my head up reading them back to You silently. I believe that You are extremely compassionate and You are willing to accept all of us as we are, as long as we come to You with our hearts open. I come to You today in this prayer with my heart open and my hand reaching for Yours. I'm knocking on Your door. I pray You give me guidance to look after everything to the best of my ability. I notice Your work every time I see a sunset, the ocean, stars, Megan, Ashley, Mom, Dad, Nanny, Deda, Mema, Papa, Lee, Tia Lynn, Rachel, a kind soul, Monica, Kelly, Kristen, Tia Ruby, Uncle Billy, and so on. I admire Your work. It is beautiful and majestic.

I tucked the letter away in a folder and tried to forget about it. A preceding course of events were about to open my eyes to how involved God was in my life. Knocking on His door was a spark to an eternal flame flickering to burn inside of me.

2

Flickering to Burn

Matthew 7:8 (NKJV)
"For everyone who asks receives, and he who seeks finds, and to him who knocks it will be opened."

My life has been on the verge of balancing between two opposing parallels since birth. Life and death, light and darkness, good and evil. Throughout my whole life, these forces have been pressing within and outside of me. The pull between those parallels forced me to choose for which one I wanted to live.

I was dating the love of my life for six months. Her name was Megan Thompson. We met in the Volusia Mall where we worked across from each other. I worked at a calendar stand for Waldenbooks, and she worked at a jewelry stand. There was a couple that worked with her who kept trying to get her to date their friend. They wanted him to breakup with his girlfriend because they thought she was too young for him.

One day, Megan pointed to me and said she would like to get to know me. She said this to get them to stop asking her to date their friend. She did not know that they knew me and would start using their matchmaking skills with us. They invited Megan and I to a party one night with them and another couple. We were riding in the backseat of their car together. I was really nervous and quiet, and my friend was trying to get me to kiss her. I could not even speak. Megan asked me what my tattoo was to break the ice.

I said, "Black Flag," and did not follow it up with another word. It was really awkward, and Megan thought I was a pirate. The party was a bust (no one was there). We went back to my friend's house, and all the couples started arguing. Megan asked me why they were arguing. I was wondering the same thing, and this started a lifelong conversation and relationship.

We actually noticed each other before the matchmakers went to work. She was going to get lunch, and we made eye contact. In her eyes there was a deep beauty, a love, a gentleness, and a quietness that I understood. The first time I looked into her eyes, it felt like everything melted away. As if the world stopped and all that existed was us. It seemed like she could see into my soul, the things I had been through, like she understood, like we had known each other our whole lives.

That moment took place in a matter of seconds. Megan showed me and continues to show me a genuine love. A love that was amazing and scary at the same time. Not really knowing it until we met, I was scared of love. Not of love itself, but the rejection and abandonment that would be felt if love decided to leave.

The root of this fear took hold at a tender age, around two. My parents decided that it was better for them to separate, and my father left. When he departed, an emptiness took his place. I will always have it. These days, I am realizing that I have choices on what to do with it. Harm is not the only choice. The choice of harmony resides just as strong, if not stronger. I would never want to go back and change my circumstances. They made me who I am.

If the divorce did not happen, my mom would have never married my stepdad. My sister would have never been born. We would not have moved from Key West to Daytona Beach. I would have not discovered surfing. This story would have been much different than the one you are reading. I would never have met Megan or built the bond I now have with my grandparents and my mom. I was still able to have beautiful moments with my dad. These good things which took place in the aftermath of divorce, I could not see as an adolescent or a teenager. I rebelled against God and authority.

My destructive ways started off small and later became entangled in my life. So much that I could not find my way out. In school, it went from skipping, to suspension, to failing classes, to getting held back a year. With drugs, it went from cigarettes, to beer, to marijuana, to LSD, to mushrooms, Rohypnol, snorting methadone, huffing Freon, and fighting urges to try heroin. Thank God that heroin was hard for me to get in Daytona Beach at the time. With sex, it went from pornography, to losing my virginity at the age of fifteen, to promiscuity, to sexual addictions, including picking up prostitutes on Ridgewood Avenue.

In the year of 1999, before I reached the age of twenty-one, these dark necessities were going on heavy in my life. The consequences were also unraveling effects of the lifestyle. I had already been arrested once, detained many times for underage drinking and possession, and was already moving through the process of programs issued by the state and community service. Honestly, I do not know how I stayed alive to meet Megan. I wanted to pick up the shards of my life and do right for her. It hurt her to see me hurt myself with alcohol and drugs. One night, I could feel the depths of my plight while walking to Megan's apartment.

I felt helpless and unsure of how to get free from all my demons. Deep down in my soul, I could feel God telling me that I was not alone. There was a stillness in my center, down in my guts, that seemed to make ripples in my mind with the words that I could come to Him and He would help me. It was not loud, but all of me was listening to it. I came to him the best way I knew how. I wrote the letter, hid it in a folder, and tried to forget about it.

3

At the Main Street Pier

There I was, pulling into the parking lot next to the Main Street Pier with one of my drug buddies. The term "drug buddies" means that our relationship had revolved around getting high. If we were to take drugs out of the equation, we barely knew each other. In fact, I cannot remember his name. I do remember that he was experimenting with heroin and had a way of getting it. We were parked in front of a raging ocean, and I could hear him talking in the distance about partying; however, another sound was commanding all of my attention: that thunderous sound the ocean makes when it is unsettled.

The ocean was all the way up to the sea wall. Not seeing sand on a beach is a rare sight. It means the ocean is aggravated. The waves were rising and crashing into the sea, churning water into white caps and foam. It resembled a washing machine. The pier was shaking, and no one was paddling out. Good conditions for me: big, scary, and no crowd. I told my buddy I was going surfing. We went to my house, smoked some bowls (marijuana smoked in a pipe), grabbed my surfboard, I dropped him off and went back to Main Street.

When I got there, it was still a massive movement of water. I stood on the beach south of the pier and planned my entrance into the madness. The ocean was in such disarray that there was no way of knowing which way the current was flowing. There was something I noticed that would help me plan my paddle out. On the south side, the waves were breaking in sets, more organized and had a better shape than the north side. The south side was the spot.

I started running into the ocean, knowing that on one side of the pier the current was moving toward it and on the other side, away from it. I was hoping I chose the latter, and I did. The moment I started to feel good about my choice, I heard, "Surfer, get out of the water and surf on the north side." This was coming from the lifeguards who, from what they could see, thought their advice was safe for me. The ocean's discord caused a perimeter around the pier. In that perimeter, all the water was sucking into the pier. The lifeguards were mistaken that the perimeter was the current. This put me in danger. I knew this, so I walked as far north from the pier as I could. This way I would have enough room to paddle out past the pier and drift south of it.

I realized a different perspective once I changed my position. I was no longer standing on the beach; I was paddling in the ocean while those liquid mountains were trying to crash on my head. Time stood still during this moment. Time standing still was different this time than when I met Megan. Meeting Megan was a love thing; this was a survival thing. I once read a book called Get in the Van. In that book, Henry Rollins described a fight he was in. He said that it felt like being in a vacuum where everything within the moment moved in slow motion. I could relate to this in a roaring sea. My main focus was getting out past the pier. During this time, something amazing started to happen, something supernatural.

4

Something Supernatural

Several months prior, my dad passed away, and I went to my birthplace to attend his funeral. My grandmother told me that his liver produced a toxin that went through his blood stream. If I was to write the full circumstances on to how he died this way, I would have another book. My guess is that there was a time when he was involved with intravenous heroin use, which could have led to him contracting a form of hepatitis, and heavy alcohol use when he was younger would have also had an effect on his liver. His life was not all of this, but I believe that the small part of his life that was had an effect on his death. Only him and God really know how and why he went.

In the graveyard, I convinced myself that God did not exist, thinking it was more feasible for Him not to exist than to exist and let this happen. I said in my mind, God, I do not believe in you. I was mad at Him. I went back to Daytona Beach the next day and had to play a show that night. I was a singer in a punk band named LBO, and we were jamming at a place called Robbie O'Connell's. In the middle of our set, something crazy started to happen. It felt as if I was in the distance with the crowd watching myself sing. Whatever emotion I felt, I let out in the music. The crowd would feed off those emotions, and I would feed off the crowd's emotions.

I was watching all of this happen as if I was an outsider. I could see myself spewing hate, anger, and resentment into the crowd, and they were sending theirs back. We were creating an environment, a hostile one.

Within a flash, I was no longer in the crowd. I was singing in front of them, not liking the idea that I had a part in creating this environment.

5

Under the Main Street Pier

Several months later, in that raging sea at the Main Street Pier, I was experiencing a similar situation in a different way. As I was paddling out, I would think of what was special to me: my family, friends, and Megan. With these thoughts, a clear path cut through the ocean. I was being helped. My arms could not move as fast as my movement, and the waves were crashing all around me. It would have looked like me paddling out in a stream that was moving me where I needed to be. In that stream, it was peaceful and calm. Outside of that stream was chaos and turbulence. Thinking of thoughts that brought anger, frustration, lust, grudges, fighting, pornography, and shameful images of my past would push me out of that stream of peace and into a sea of sorrow. The ocean was picking itself up and crashing on my head.

Every attempt to move forward would result in me moving backward. The ocean was more powerful than my efforts. I tried to switch my thoughts back and forth, from good to bad and bad to good. Every time I would think good, the stream of peace. Every time I would think bad, the sea of sorrow and chaos. That sorrow and chaos was wearing me thin, so I tried to focus just on good. During these tries, bad thoughts would creep in. This struggle continued until I was out past the pier drifting to the south of it. I was far enough out to be away from the perimeter, but I was still out in front of the pier.

If I got any closer to the shore, there was a danger of me getting into the perimeter and getting sucked into the pier. A wave was building in the distance. It was one of those rogue waves that broke bigger and farther out than the rest. I was off to the races, paddling as fast as my arms could move. It did not work; the wave broke with power and ferocity. I tried to duck dive (when a surfer pushes their surfboard under the water to get them and their board under a wave).

The breaking wave was too big for me to get under, and it washed me into a place where I would not have voluntarily wanted to be in my whole life's experience of being in the ocean. The wave pulled me into the depths of the sea, feeling the cold darkness, not sure which way was up or down, starting to panic, not knowing what to do and feeling my life slipping away while struggling to breathe. I just remembered that when a wave gets a hold of you, there is no fighting it. Fighting would expend the energy I would need to swim to the surface once the wave let me go. After that thought, my tension relieved, a rush of water sprang under my feet and shot me up to the surface. I broke through the surface, gasping for air.

The perimeter was surrounding me, and I could feel the ocean pulling me into the pier. A wave equally as big as the last one was swelling on the horizon. The wave broke with sheer force. I knew that if I could not duck dive under the wave, it would push me through the pier backward.

There was no way I was going on that ride backward. I wanted to at least see what I was going through. I turned around to ride the wave on my stomach and face the pier head on. The poles that hold the pier up became outstretched pillars that I needed to dodge. With the shifting of my weight to the left or the right, I would fly past each pole.

The wave died out and left me directly under the restaurant, the widest and worst part to be stuck in. I was surrounded by poles in every direction. Another wave was on its way, and there was no escaping the poles. I hit two poles in the middle of the pier, paddled to the north side and got sucked into two more poles by the dreaded perimeter. I made it to shore, immediately walked up to the lifeguard tower, and gave them the bird. It was not the bird with wings. I am glad that they did not come out. A fight or a possible jail visit was not something I needed to add to the situation. I was alive. I made it out alive. I looked over my body, and there was not one scratch on it.

The conditions of the ocean were harsh enough to show me how small I was in comparison to its mass. With one stir of it, I could have easily slammed into the pier and broken to pieces or drowned out in front of it. To my surprise, the conditions were also set up in a way to protect me from its onslaught. The tide was so high that the water was above the barnacles on the poles. Barnacles are often so jagged that just a firm touch could slice open skin. The wood of the poles was all I hit, and there seemed to be a buffer around each pole.

Even though the perimeter around the pier was working against me, there was what seemed to be a perimeter around the poles that was working for me. The water was sucking into each pole and pushing outward. Every time I washed into a pole, I would hit that perimeter which, in turn, buffered me from slamming into it. Coming out of that situation was a miracle. I just did not see it yet.

The same night of the incident LBO was practicing at our drummer Justin Bradford's house. We would always start off with a song called "Undertow." I wrote "Undertow" around a year prior to that night. The song was about my partying lifestyle and how partying was a way for me to check out of reality.

The only problem was that the problems were still waiting for me when I checked back into reality. Not to mention I had new problems that were often added from the party. This was affecting my life in a way to where I felt like I was barely keeping my head above water. That song was Justin's mom's favorite, so it would always be first on the playlist of our jam sessions.

Undertow

So here I am reaching out
Of the water so I don't drown
All these thoughts are racing through my brain
So here I am not too proud
My pride has dropped and hit the ground
I see what I lost and what I didn't gain
So, I take this little ride and go to a place where I can hide
Cause I feel I'm breaking down
So here I am with this thorned up crown
I'm still amongst the same old crowd
I'll leave there's so much more to prove
So, I take this little ride and go to a place where I can hide
Cause I feel I'm breaking down

6

A Song, Opened Eyes, and Miracles

The band started in with this building then driving groove. I chimed in with the first verse: "So here I am reaching out of the water so I don't drown." As I was singing those words, I could not help but realize, I just lived out that song hours earlier. I remembered the letter I wrote to the Lord. I told Justin's parents about the letter and the pier, knowing they were close to God. Mr. Bradford said, "Well, you asked to see God, and you saw Him." We talked about God and prayed before I went home. It felt so good talking to God in that prayer.

In my letter when I asked to see God, I thought it would take one moment. I did not know He was so deep with so many different dimensions that it would take a lifetime of seeing all the segments of who He was. In this lifetime I would not completely fathom Him, because my finite shell of a body could not handle the fullness of who He was. For my own safety, I would have to see Him in doses.

In the following days, the Lord started to reveal in my memories how He was always with me. He was gently and patiently arranging situations in my life that were preparing me for the moment when I would turn my attention to Him. He knew me from the depths of my insides. The places I would try to hide from everyone else, because this was where I was most vulnerable. In the depths, I started opening up to see Him.

I could see Him in a story my grandma used to tell me. My mom was pregnant with me and wanted to go fishing with my dad and his friends. My grandmother tried to convince my mom not to go, because she was so close to delivery. My mom was set on going, but decided not to go in the last minute. The boat flipped that night, and my dad and his friends were left stranded at night in the middle of the ocean, getting burns on their skin from the hot fuel. God was protecting me while I was still in the womb.

I saw that it was not by chance that all my friends around me were getting to know Him and sharing their stories with me. Or, that Justin's parents were at our band practice that night. Or, that I would take these walks around a pond to get stoned. On many of those walks, I would feel a presence within and around me that would sober me up from the weed. Like, when my friends and I were drinking all night and started talking about God. The same feeling and presence that came in reaction to our discussion sobered us up and was greater than any substance we could have taken. It was Him. I realized there was a reason why I heard the name of Jesus so many times in my life. It was God reaching out through the name of His Son.

I could see Him in the night when I drank so much mushroom tea that I thought I died from AIDS. I tried to call my friends in warning, but I could not reach them. That night, I saw that I wasted my life on partying and never got to live my dreams. I was stuck in my sin, running around in circles, in desolation, naked in the streets, trying to find heaven, knowing it was too late, because I was dead. I laid down in the streets that night thinking that it would take me out of the hell I was in. A car stopped right in front of me. I tasted hell that night. I came to in a police station where I was being charged with grand theft auto of a police car and disorderly conduct. God was with me.

Second Letter (Early 2002)

Jesus Christ,

It's me again. I praise You for showing me Your light. I will bathe in it and purify myself with Your spirit. I thank You for touching everyone's soul, and I pray those who are lost will feel your gentle hands upon their hearts. I pray that You shield Justin, Anthony, Brad, Mike, Pat, Megan, and myself from the devil's work. I ask that You forgive me for my sins. In the name of the Father, the Son, the Spirit, and the Holy Ghost.

7

A Closer Walk

The Lord had my attention. I knew how involved He was in my life, even when I was not involved in His. The glimpse of who He was had me wanting more. After praying with the Bradfords, I realized that prayer was a start. I would talk to God as a friend. When I was happy, mad, sad, content with the feeling of His presence, or not feeling Him at all, I would talk to Him. During those talks, I could sense a strong desire to get a Bible.

The first time I could remember picking up a Bible was around six months before the letter. I was at the optometrist, and there was a Bible in the waiting room. I started to read the first page in the book of Genesis. It blew my mind. I never knew that the things we see in the world—the light, grass, sky, the land, and the seas—were all spoken to existence through God's words, and there I was reading God's words. Who would have known that the things that grow have a seed God put within them to reproduce in the likeness of themselves or that God shaped man from the dust of the earth? He breathed His life into man. I was amazed, completely amazed.

I needed to find a Bible and prayed to God for one. I worked in a convention center called the Ocean Center at the time. One day, I went to the cage where we would get supplies and take breaks. Inside the cage, I saw all of these bibles left behind from a recent church convention. I started to read one of those bibles on my breaks. The lady I worked with would always say, "You better take one, Anthony; no one's coming back for them." I did not want to take someone's Bible. I did want a Bible to read until I got my own, so I continued reading those in the cage. I never felt that way reading any other book.

Most of my life I had spent seeking the truth, looking for it in books, movies, music, surfing, drugs, relationships, sex, and alcohol. I finally found it. It was like God's truth was speaking directly to my heart. Those stories in it were about God's relationship with His people: Moses, David, Elijah, Naomi, Ruth, Samson, Peter, and Paul. He had the same relationship with me. All of those men and women were broken and made many mistakes in life. Just like me. That Bible was God's love letter to me through the testimonies of people who walked with Him in the past.

One night I went to the Bradfords with Megan, and Mrs. Bradford gave us bibles. This was an answered prayer. It made me so happy! I would take these trips with my Bible, my skateboard, and just enough money to ride the bus around town. I would sit down at a bus stop and read my Bible until the bus came. I would catch the bus and ride it wherever it went. If I saw a place that I liked, I would get off and explore.

During these excursions, I noticed something about the people around me while reading the Bible. Some people would get extremely uncomfortable, fidgety, give me dirty looks, and sometimes they just got up and left. There were also moments when a person would just sit next to me and stay as close as they could while I was reading. It was like they were hanging on to the moment; I was too. Those moments were really special and helped me see how good God was. Those glimpses were mending my relationship with Him, on my side. On His side, He was always the same, pure love.

Poem During the Time (Early 2002)

You were with me in the darkness of waters
Knitting pieces of me into existence
Breathing Your life's breath into my soul
And we danced
Feeling the pain around me
Blaming it on you
Turned my head and walked away
To do what I wanted to do
And you danced
Consuming all to fill an emptiness
That only existed out of your presence
My world was spinning out of my control
You placed others around me
They pointed to you
And you danced
In desperation I reached for your hand
A touch made me whole again
The warmth of your face
Shining brighter than the sun
Filling me with light and love
Now we dance

After that poem, I stopped writing songs and poems. It was weird; the need to write them stopped. I was not even concerned about it. This used to be a way for me to express what was going on deep inside of me. It was a way to work things out. The letters to God kept flowing, though.

Letter During the Time (Early 2002)

I thank You, Lord, for always being with me. For never leaving me. I owe You all that I am and it still would not compare to what You have done for me.

> Psalm 139:17–18 (NKJV)
> "How precious also are your thoughts to me, oh God! How great is the sum of them! If I should count them, they would be more in number than the sand; when I awake, I am still with You."

The band was slowly unraveling. We did not practice that much and the times we did were not the same. There was a rift. I think we all could feel that the band was going in three different directions. We all knew we could not walk together on separate paths. I did not have the courage to share what I felt with the rest of the band. I loved those guys and did not want to be confronted with the truth that our band might break up.

My life was slowly unraveling as well. The things that I spent the most time trying to hold onto were slipping from my grip. I was losing music, writing, my friends, and I had peace for some reason. My extra time and energy were being spent on seeking the Lord. I just knew that somehow God was looking out for my best interest. I was feeling His love in a deep beautiful way and that was what was important. I just had a feeling that everything would work out.

There was a guy I worked with at the Ocean Center named Brad. Brad was a drummer in a band that would play and practice with our band. He was also a close friend. One day, while we were working, I told him about the letter, the pier, and how I was starting out this adventure with God. While I was telling him my story, I could see the excitement in his eyes. It was like he was waiting to hear that story the whole time he knew me. Then it all started to click.

A few months earlier, Mikey, the singer in Brad's band, pointed out something about Brad. Every time something would happen in our lives where we dodged jail or death, Brad would say, "Hey, did you see that? That was crazy." We did not really understand why he would say that. After telling Brad my story, I realized he had a story of his own. I could see my conversation with Mikey was about Brad showing us the times when God was intervening in our lives. He was calling it out. Brad lived with his two older brothers and no parents. I had a feeling his story would be special.

When Brad was young, his mom died of cancer. He remembered that in the last days of her life, she would always have praise and worship music on. She would sing those songs and Brad said that he would feel the presence of God fill the hospital room. Before she died, she gathered the three boys together and told them to always look out for each other. She told them to believe in God and know that He will always be with them and that she was going to be with Jesus. After she passed, Brad's father would not take custody of the boys. Brad's older brothers raised him from that day on, like Ponyboy from the Outsiders movie.

My new Bible continued to occupy my time. I started off reading the smaller books like Habakkuk, the Gospels, and then I went straight for the beginning, Genesis. Mr. Bradford told me that his father once set out to read the full Bible so he would know everything. He figured if he could read the Bible in full, he would learn everything there was to know. It turned out that when he was done, he realized he knew nothing. Knowing this story, I wanted to read the whole Bible and come to the same realization. My knowledge was getting me into trouble anyway. The process of unlearning would give me a new beginning, a clean slate.

I would read in my backyard, during breaks at work, before surfing, my bus excursions, even while smoking pot. God would teach me lessons and show me who He was and who I was through His Word. All of my thoughts and ways of seeing the world were different from the world's view around me. This made me feel like an alien. It was something that became a part of my search for the truth. Why was I so different? God's word was the way I thought. It was in me from a young age. It was my identity. It was who I was. I just did not know it until I read it.

I was smoking some bowls and reading my Bible on the porch one day when my little sister walked up and questioned what I was doing. She was wondering why I was smoking pot and reading the Bible at the same time. I told her I loved God and was trying to get to know Him by reading the Bible. I also told her that quitting drugs was not easy for me. Deep down, I knew that I loved drugs as well, and there was something in me that did not want to sever ties with it. When my sister left, I read a story where Jesus was talking about being an influence on the younger generation. He said to lead one child astray was like tying a huge rock around your neck and being thrown into the sea.

I realized that although Ashley would never say it, she did look up to me. I was her older brother, and my conflicted lifestyle was probably hard for her to understand. I was a contradictory example before her eyes. My relationship with drugs was taking a toll on my relationship with God and the people I loved. Drugs were taking more from me than they were giving. Staying in town was not helping me kick my habits either. I needed desperately to leave my town to quit drugs. I prayed for it.

8

My Exodus

There was a man Brad and I worked with named Marty. He would try to help us in our quest to leave Daytona Beach. His one way for us to leave was to join the military. I would tell him thanks but no thanks—not for me.

My paradigm toward the military was this. It was a rich man's way of recruiting a poor man, because he knew the poor man was limited in ways of getting out of his situation. My thoughts were that if the poor man could not afford school, then the rich man would offer the poor man school and money to fight his wars. I wondered why the kids who joined and Marty could not see this. Marty argued that we would get out of town and learn a trade.

Brad was taking the bait. Brad thought it would be a good idea for us to join the military together, move out to California, and start a band. He was seriously thinking about this and talking to his brothers about it. I told Brad to pray and see what God would say.

Meanwhile, I was reading the Bible on my porch one day, and I could feel a nudge, a pressing from God, that He wanted me to join. I closed the Bible, put it down, and could not believe it. I could not shake it. I told the Lord that day He knew what was best. I told Him I would do it, but I wanted to know this was something He wanted me to do. In the next couple weeks, He would send a random person my way each day to tell me about their experience in the military and how they wished they would have stayed to retire.

This happened every day for like a week straight. I still questioned the Lord on it, asking Him to show me that He wanted me to join. One night, I was reading the book of Exodus where God told Israel that He would go before them. He even told them that He would prepare the way for them. When I read this, I knew that God was talking directly to me in those passages. It was like He was saying, through those verses, "Look Anthony, I know what I am asking of you; do not be afraid, I will be with you, and I will even go before you to make a way." I closed the Bible and still could not shake it. Those words were speaking loud in my heart. I knew what I had to do.

What was really crazy about that time was that in the book of Exodus there was a connection with the lives of the people of Israel and my own life. I did not notice it in the moment. I can now see this in hindsight. God was calling His people, Israel, out of Egypt where they lived as slaves. He was leading them into a land He promised, the land of Canaan, where they could be free. My exodus was leaving the place of my captivity to my own sin. God was saying that He would go out of Daytona Beach and prepare a way for me to get out of my addictions. He would bring me into the place He promised.

I decided to join the Navy. One day at work, I told Brad about my decision. He said that he was not going to join. He consulted his brothers on it, and they talked him out of it. I thought that Brad would be the first one to go and that I would be the last, but to say that God moves in mysterious ways would be an understatement. He moves like the wind, and it is hard to predict or know how or where the wind will move. You just know what it is doing when you feel it.

My friends and family had mixed opinions when I told them. There was a little fear and excitement from everyone about my decision. The fear was from the unknown. During this time, America was facing the wake of September eleventh, the collapse of the Twin

Towers. There was a strong possibility that war was in our future. They definitely did not want me to be involved in a war. The excitement on their part was that there was a possibility of me moving forward into a new chapter of my life.

A chapter that would be positive for me. One that would bring changes that would lead me into adulthood. Some growing could take place. Maybe that journey would shape me into a man. I thought that Megan would try to talk me out of it like Brad's brothers did for him. I think that a part of me was hoping she would. Walking into the unknown was and still is frightening, humbling, and quite vulnerable. Trusting the Lord was key, and I had lost my trust in everyone else to some point in my life. Humans are not perfect and to put all my trust in us as a whole or even in one individually would only lead to me being let down.

I would be hurt intentionally or even non-intentionally. Good and bad comes together in every person and the good helps and the bad hurts. We're a mixed bag. Jesus is the only one that is not. He is all good. Joining the Navy was a trust fall for me. When I told Megan about it, she was extremely supportive. She told me how exciting it would be to get out and see the world.

She also knew that I needed to get away from my own ghost who was haunting me in Daytona Beach. After all, this was the place where I had my first drunken night, took my first hit of LSD, got in many fights, spent my first night in jail, lost my virginity, and lost my mind. There were many things in that town that I needed to step away from. I needed to move toward something that was pure, real, and bound in truth. Something that would leave an everlasting mark on me and the world around me. God was leading me out of my life away from Him and leading me into a life with and in Him.

I laid down on a hotel bed (paid for by the Navy) that night in Jacksonville, Florida, freaking out. The next morning, I would be going to the Military Entrance Processing Station (MEPS). This is the place where they make you walk like a duck, among other things.

Those who have been there know what I mean. At this place, they check to see if you are physically fit to join the military. If I was, I would be on my way to boot camp in two weeks. In that hotel room, my mind was reeling and stressing on the unknown. I opened my Bible, prayed to God, and asked Him for peace and guidance. I started to read about Jesus washing the feet of His disciples.

He went to each one, washing their feet in water and drying their feet with His loincloth. As I read those words, I could feel a peace coming into my heart. The Lord was also leading me to wash my own feet. I did not know why and was apprehensive, because there was a chance my roommate would walk in anytime. I placed my feet in the bathtub, started the water, the water washed over my feet. With my hands I moved the water from my heels to my toes and back and forth.

I took the towel, dried my feet, and laid back in bed. Waves of adulation washed over my body. It was the spirit of God. His spirit moved in waves like the water that washed over my feet. The Holy Spirit moved from my head to my toes and back again. This washing took away all my fears, all my worries and all my anxieties far away from me. It left me in a complete peace, with a freedom and an admiration toward the one who could do this in an instant.

The next day I went to MEPS. They had a problem with one of my scars, so I had to get the medical records sent to them. Within a few days, MEPS deemed me fit, and I was accepted into the Navy on waivers for my scar and prior charges with the law. When I signed up with the recruiter, I was not sure what job I wanted to do in the Navy. I did not have many choices because I was waived in from my past possession charge.

I asked the recruiter what he thought, and he asked if I liked to run. I said it was okay. He told me that they run a lot on the flight deck and there was this new apprenticeship program. He said that in the program, you were able to start as an airman and if you did not like your job, you could take a test (strike) for another job (rate).

This sounded good, but there was a problem with it that I learned later. That apprenticeship helped add sailors to rates that were unmanned, but most of the sailors would end up in the rate they started in. They would not strike. There were many reasons for this. One reason was that if you were a good sailor, your division would want to keep you. The division would help you with your advancement in that rate, but if you wanted a different rate, they would not want to help you.

You would have to explore those other rates in your own time and still be competitive in your own division. Years later, the rates in that apprenticeship filled up, were overmanned, and made the percentage of sailors trying to make rank usually at less than ten percent of each exam. The divisions were so overmanned that it was hard to make rank. I did not know these things when I asked my recruiter. He pitched the apprenticeship as a good idea, and I signed up to go to boot camp as an airman apprentice.

9

Boot Camp Letters

Two weeks later, I was standing in the parking lot of the recruiter's office waiting for the van to pick me up. The van arrived, I stepped into it, and watched the faces of my family and Megan fade into the distance as it drove off to the airport where I would fly to Chicago and get on a bus that would drive me to Great Lakes for boot camp. There was a deep feeling of loneliness mixed with the questions of, "What the hell am I doing this for?" and "Why Lord?" inside of me. These feelings and questions would repeat throughout my life in the Navy, especially on those drives, walks, and flights away from my family.

God would always comfort me in due time, but those drives, walks, and flights were some of the hardest things I ever had to do in my life. I flew into Chicago where a bus was waiting for me. On the bus, there were around fifteen young men from all walks of life. We had different ethnicities, different views, and different past experiences, but some of us also shared commonalities with these things. The one thing we all had in common was that we were all going to boot camp in Great Lakes, and together we would add to the bulk of our division.

The first thing I noticed on the bus was our hair. Some had real long hair like me, some came prepared with freshly shaved heads, and one guy even had a mohawk. The bus pulled in front of a building at the naval station in Great Lakes. There were around six instructors in the parking lot waiting for us like a pack of hungry dogs.

I could hear them barking when the first kid stepped off the bus. I cannot remember all that was said, but if you have ever seen the Scared Straight programs or Full Metal Jacket, it is all the same lingo.

"Get out of the bus, recruit."

"Are you eyeballin' me?"

"It is 'yes, Petty Officer' to you."

"Are you calling me petty?"

Inside of the building, we all lined up to piss in a cup and were issued some gear afterward. We were led to a hallway where we waited to get our heads freshly shaven. The lady who cut my hair was mad that my hair was so long. I often wondered what they thought about the mohawk. We went back to the hallway, sat there, and waited and waited and waited. It felt like we were in that hallway for two days.

At the end of this, we got to sleep in a wide-open room that seemed like an open hanger with nothing but bunk beds. This is the place where we were deferred until we had enough recruits for a division. After a week, we were classed up as division 221 and we got to meet our Recruit Division Commanders (RDCs).

Boot Camp Letter to Megan (April 20, 2002)

Good afternoon beautiful,

I'm writing on a Sunday afternoon on April 20. Our anniversary is in just five days. I'm sorry that I couldn't write earlier. We were not allowed to send out anything today. In fact, we started receiving mail two days ago. I will graduate and be able to leave by June 14. "Can't wrap my arms around the pictures in my head. I still got a ways to go. Until then I'll pretend. Until then I promised you, I wouldn't bend. Till then I'll spend my time waiting until then." ([2]Stevenson, Alvarez and ALL. "Until Then.") I promise I won't bend by graduating on time. Actually, I will see you before that if you visit me on Liberty weekend. I'm allowed to invite three people. Guess who I invited? You, Ashley, and Mom. The greatest family one could have.

On some forms I filled out, I listed you as my fiancé. Boot camp is getting a little more relaxed. We still get beat (working out a lot), when a certain group of kids won't be quiet. Our RDCs are tough sometimes, but if we listen to them, "We will be a very good division." We won't get beat. We would just train. I'm learning how to iron and fold clothes. I bet you would have never thought I would be saying that. I'm learning how to fold my bunk.

These are the hardest things I've done. I'm learning slowly, however. Our division is 221, so tell Mom to play that for cash three. The food we ate is pretty good. It makes everyone fart. Since we all eat the same food, all our farts smell the same. If twenty guys fart, it is like one massive fart. It's terrible. You can't escape it when you're marching either. There are eighty-three guys in our division. There were eighty-six, but three guys got ASMO'ed (dropped to another division, they graduate later).

I have been keeping you in my prayers every day and keeping you in my thoughts every second. You are my strength sweetie. The strength on your back is contagious, and it transfers to my back every time I think of you. When the RDCs are yelling, I go to my happy place, the jetty at Ponce. This is how I picture it. Rocks stretching out between two endless spaces. The sea and the sky. There are stars in the sky and the ocean. The oceans stars are blue, the reflection of your eyes.

We are standing on the rocks, hand in hand. The light in your smile fills me with happiness. We are trying to pick out a path. There are awkward rocks all around us, but in the middle, there is a clear-cut path to where the ocean and the sky meet. The light around us is mesmerizing, but even more so within us. We are cuddling, whispering, and kissing. The RDC's voice is just a blade of grass when I'm in my happy spot.

Tell everyone I'm thinking about them and to write me if they can. Get the address off the front and please send me some letters. I would like to know how you are doing. You can write anything you want because the RDCs don't go through them. I miss you so much, and you are always on my heart.

Boot Camp Letter to Megan (April 22, 2002)

Angel,

How are you doing? I miss you so much. You are the light of my life. Every time I get discouraged in this place, remembering your smile helps me smile. You still make my day even when you're in a different state. This place is wild. Our RDCs are tough on us only when they have to be which is often. I met some really nice kids. I try to stay around the ones that make the RDCs happy, because when they're happy everyone's happy. If they're not happy, a sullen vibe falls over the group and everyone turns grumpy. The deodorant they issued me smells like you.

It makes me happy every time I put it on. All of the recruits that have been here before us say that this is the worst part and it gets much easier. I look at your picture every night. We have what they call a valuable sock. In the sock we put our valuables so I put you in my sock. I also keep the cross in there, because I can't wear it. Every time I see that picture, I think about you surfing with me.

I remember how happy you were when you stood up for the first time. It was cute how you kept asking me if I saw it and that smile, oh how it polishes my thoughts. Well, I better get some sleep. I love you more than every beat of every heart.

Boot Camp Letter to Megan (May 06, 2002)

Hello my love,

I am writing you from the depths of my heart and the body within my body, my soul. Each morning before I wake up, my soul is starting its journey to a distant place south from here. During this journey I am not complete. Half of me is amiss. There is a time in the day every day when that emptiness vanishes. This is the time when I realize that my soul wasn't the only one making that journey. Your soul reaches me and lets me know that my soul has reached you. At this moment the light shines from the heavens. It touches me and everything around me.

This is when I see signs such as: peanut butter, oranges (by the way, I eat oranges and PBJs everyday), a Daytona sky in Chicago, the birds playing in the bushes, the trees on the base that have pink flowers and toward the top of the trees the flowers have pink and white. It looks like the trees are holding snow. It is so beautiful. This is when I know that the Lord has truly blessed me with your presence.

I'm sure you're probably wondering how things are going for me in boot camp. I passed my first three inspections (barely). I got three hits on each inspection. If you get four, you fail. I also passed my test with a 3.6, and you need a 2.7 to pass. I'm trying to get way better on both these areas. Things are going a little smoother like folding and my studying. I have some really cool clothes.

My first issue was four utility shirts and pants (those are the baby blue shirts we saw in my DEP book). The pants are just like Dickies except a little thicker and my name is on the back pocket. I also have a jacket with Velcro, a zipper, and my last name is on the chest pocket. It is a rain jacket. It is really cool. I got two pairs of navy sweats and New Balance sneakers. I have a pair of steel toe boots. You can walk through puddles and your feet don't even get wet; they are waterproof. I also have a long black trench coat with an inside that zippers into it in case the weather is cold.

I have the army glasses. They are just what I expected. They're really cool. I also have undershirts, whitey tighties, a hat, and a beanie. My second issue was the white sailor outfit and the black one. I really like the black one. When we got our first issue, I was just wearing underwear under my pants. We were supposed to have our PT shorts on also. It wasn't a pretty situation. I made sure I was wearing them for my second issue.

I also have a pea coat. It has really big buttons. I feel like James Dean when I put it on. I went to church on my first free Sunday. It seemed like the preacher mixed the Navy with the church in the wrong way. He told us that we made a vow with God when we joined the Navy and we can't run from that vow. It was a powerful sermon, and I could feel the spirit was there. In my opinion, he could have made a better approach to kids who just went through a hundred-and-eighty-degree change in their life.

I haven't been to church since, basically because I fell behind a little bit the time I went. It took me a week to catch up. I have been reading the Bible: Corinthians, Thessalonians, Colossians, and Numbers have been the books of interest for me. Every time I read, the Lord speaks to me through the Word for the situation I'm going through. God is amazing! I am getting very sleepy. I'm signing off. Tell your mom thanks for the letters. They were encouraging and not to worry because I'm going to make it through. I will try to write her back if I get the time. Your letters are so wonderful. When I open them, magic fills the room. I love you so much. I wish you the best of dreams.

Boot Camp Letter to Megan (May 15, 2002)

> "Our bed we live, our bed we sleep, sharing orange blossom breezes. Stabbing thorns and naked feet, I become you, you become me, oh. I beg for you. Take a bath I'll drink the water that you leave. If you should die before me ask if you could bring a friend."
> ([3]Weiland and Stone Temple Pilots. "Still Remains.")

Hi my lovely angel,

Guess what I saw yesterday morning? I saw an orange and purple sunrise. Our two favorite colors blending perfectly, just as our lives have blended perfectly ever since we kissed under the tree in Mickey's backyard. It made my day. It was wonderful. When I called you, I felt the same way as you. Things are going good in boot camp. I had four inspections and one written test the past week. Two of my inspections I didn't get any hits and the other one I only got one hit.

Our other inspection was a team inspection on marching, we won a flag on it. They give flags to the divisions that score high on the inspection or test they are given. Three flags in all; all the flags we could win for that week, we won. One of the kids in my division said that we scored higher than any division in the past thirteen years on the written test. I'm not sure what my score was, but I feel pretty confident that I passed it. I've been going to church the past two Sundays.

Last Sunday, the preacher was talking about the same verse that I got in your card that had the two pair of shoes. I just got that card two days ago. Those connections we share are amazing. You travel with me when I march through this base. The thought of you blowing kisses in your sleep elevates me. You are so beautiful, wonderful, the love of my life, and the light of my life.

I love you so much Angelfish.

Love, Ant

~~~

Boot Camp Letter to Megan (May 28, 2002)

Hi my beautiful love dove,

How are you doing, my sweet pea? The card with the letter with the butterfly was beautiful. All of the cards you send me are beautiful, kind, sweet, and thoughtful. You are a true blessing in my life. The time when we will be in each other's arms is close to my touch, taste, and smell. The other day I filled out my dream sheet of places I'd like to be stationed at. The three places I chose were: first–Mayport, second–California, third–Texas. I chose Mayport because that way we could be close and you could finish school.

I chose California second because it sounds like a really neat place and there's plenty of good schools if you would like to join me. Third, I chose Texas because it was the closest place on the list to Florida. North Carolina wasn't on the list. I'm sorry sweetie. The overseas places I chose were Spain first, Italy second, and Hawaii third. I chose those for France and the waves. We should get our orders within a week. This week we had a fast cruise. Fast cruise is when every person within their division in their fifth week gets to work a certain job for seven days. I was in the scullery, washing dishes.

I was the A-captain, second person in charge. It was pretty cool. I will tell you about it when I see you. Oh, do I have some stories to tell. There are a lot of tricks I'm learning in the Navy, and each passing day is a closing in the gap of our separation. When we are united, I will give you the biggest hug ever. We won another flag! I'm really tired so I'm going to crash and dream of you. By the way, I had a dream I was in the mall with Scotty, Sammy, and Mike. They were all arguing about their girlfriends and I was like, "Give me a break," and the whole time there was a silhouette of you walking outside of my dream.

It was like those glass balls with the cities under water and when you shake the water the snow covers the city. You were the snow, and the mall was the city. I hope you understand the analogy. I love you with every motion of every cell in my body.

Hugs and kisses, Ant.

During the process of writing this book I sat in my living room with those old boot camp letters spread all around me, trying to figure out how they fit into my story. Reading them released emotions and memories that I forgot I had. There were also many emotions and memories that were not in the letters, but they were unraveled through the letters. I started to remember the red lights at night and the restless sleep.

It felt like a dream on a reel playing over and over that was filled with those same red lights mixed with the screams of recruits and RDCs drilling in the middle of the night because discrepancies were found. I can remember staring at the frames that housed the glass windows in our barracks during our inspections. The frames were the shape of crosses and staring at those crosses would help me stand still while at attention during inspections.

I can remember young men getting together and helping each other learn how to iron and fold in the middle of the night. I can remember the jokes, the laughs, and singing songs together. I can also remember us crying and yelling at each other like brothers. I can remember being so tired after battle stations that it felt like I was marching in step while sleeping. I can remember one day we were getting beat so hard that it felt like the room was perspiring and raining down on us. That day the RDCs brought out the flag and had us all hold it up while the song "I'm Proud to be an American" was played. I can still feel the emotions that were released by my fellow recruits that day. I feel that there is a big misconception toward veterans.

I feel like many people think that when we are fighting for our country that is what we are thinking about. I know as a veteran that I was not thinking about my country in the midst of heavy situations and my moments were not near as heavy as most veterans. I believe that the heavier the moment, the more my thoughts would have been focused just on the moment. That is the only way to make it out safe.

You can get hurt thinking of what is going on thousands of miles away. You have to save it for your rest time and dreams. When I was in it, I was thinking of the men and women who were in it with me. My thoughts were on them, and I know their thoughts were on me. We focused on how to make it through each situation together and get each other out in one piece. Our families were waiting for us back home.

I would hear the stories from my friends in the Navy about their families. I would feel a deep connection with their families as well after hearing the countless stories we would tell each other. In the thick of it, it is not about the rights, the freedom, the flag, the land. It is about your brothers and sisters that are out there with you in the middle of the ocean. It is about being there for them and knowing that they are there for you. It is about taking care of each other and working together to accomplish something that is bigger than one individual and to get back home. Hoping those same things, we were learning together we could bring back home. Hoping that the tight-knit community, the closeness, the teamwork would spread into the nation that we were fighting for, and my most important goal was to reunite with my family that was waiting for me.

I received my orders and was stationed on the aircraft carrier (Abraham Lincoln, CVN 72) in Everett, Washington. That was definitely not a choice on my list. Those orders put me almost as far as I could be from my family and friends. I graduated boot camp on time and got to see Megan, Ashley, and my mom on Liberty weekend, the only time in boot camp when families were allowed to visit.

I would have a two-week A-school to learn what I would be doing on the ship. I did not know that there were five divisions in the same air department that I was going to. There was V-1 which was the Aviation Boatswain's Mate Handling (ABH). They were the directors of aircraft on the flight deck. There was V-2, and they were Aviation Boatswain's Mate Equipment (ABEs). They worked on the catapults that launched aircraft. They also worked on the arresting gear that caught aircraft when they landed. Then you had V-3, which were ABHs who directed aircraft in the hangar bay. V-4 was Aviation Boatswain Mate Fuel (ABFs), and they fueled aircraft. V-5 could be ABHs, ABEs or ABFs, and they worked up in the tower with the Air Boss and Mini Boss. They kept track of what aircraft were launching and landing on the flight deck. They also kept track of which aircraft were in the pattern in the sky.

The A-school that I was going to was about a two-week crash course which would teach each airman apprentice the fundamentals of each division. We did not know which division we would be in until we got to the fleet. After my A-school, I would have some time off for leave then I was off to the fleet. The day I got to the base, the Masters at Arms (MAs) gave me a ride to the ship. On the way, they said, "Do you know that you are going on a deployment in a few days?" I had no clue.

The MAs dropped me off, and I could not believe how massive the Lincoln was. I could not imagine how something so gigantic could float. I remember talking with a friend about the experience of walking onto that ship for the first time. He related it to walking into the belly of a beast. I walked over the brow, into the insides of the ship, and onto the quarterdeck. I did not know what division I was in, so the person on watch called the Air Department to send a representative.

A Second-Class Petty Officer from V-3 came to take me to the office where I would pick my division. When we got there, they said that my two choices were V-2 and V-3. My representative told me that if I went to V-2, I would never sleep and to pick V-3. I picked V-3. I finally had my division and was ready to leave in the next few days on a cruise that would be longer than nine months. None of us knew this yet. We all thought the cruise would last six months.

10

Lincoln Letters

Culmination of Letters to God while stationed on the Abraham Lincoln (CVN 72) from 2002-2007:

July 19, 2002 (Lincoln Letters)

Dear Heavenly Father,
    It amazes me just to see the work You do. The work You do inside of me, outside of me, and through me. You have placed me in the center of Your majestic word and work yesterday. I am in the town that You have laid your gentle hand upon. Seattle, Washington and Everett are truly amazing and beautiful. This town is blossoming in Your work. Hillside villages, a city behind beautiful water, and behind the city are wonderful mountains. I pray that You will protect Meg and I, so we'll be able to explore this beautiful countryside when I get back.

After this letter, we started what would become a nine-and a half month deployment (July 2002–May 2003) in support of Operation Iraqi Freedom.

July 23, 2002 (Lincoln Letters)

I just talked to Meg and Mom. I praise You for the blessing of being able to hear their voices. I'm sitting at a bus stop in California, looking for a way to the beach. My first impression of Cali was a huge version of Daytona except there's mountains and cliffs. I'm extremely excited to be blessed by You to explore it. I pray that You bless my adventure and the hearts of those who are in my heart. Last night I had trouble sleeping because the kid above my bunk said he hates his wife and he's going to kill himself. I thank You, Lord, for sending his friend to keep him in his rack until help arrived. Forgive me where I have failed You, my Lord.

There was a time last night where I was more worried about my sleep than this poor kid who was going through a tough time. Every word is important. Every word is looking for a home. Thank You, Lord, I am now on a bus heading toward Imperial Beach. I am now on the Imperial Beach pier. You have provided a beautiful day for the Californians and us tourists. A pier performer is playing "I Don't Want to Wait in Vain" (Bob Marley). He is really good. He has a drum machine and everything.

I'll take a picture of the beach and the performer for my lovely Megan and my beautiful family. The ocean is near the shore, and I am suspended above it. Blue cascading chords would set any mind at ease, relaxing every bone, and filling empty stomachs. Singing, dancing, wishing I could share this moment.

August 1, 2002 (Lincoln Letters)

I love You so much. When I feel distant, I always come to the conclusion that You are standing next to me. I praise You, Lord. I thank You for the most remarkable blessing. That blessing is Megan.

When she is gone my mind is with her and I feel lonely. I praise You for being able to talk to her.

Between August 1, 2002 and August 16, 2002

    Nothing much really happened. A lot of work. Almost fourteen hours a day and seven days a week. I got four qualifications, thanks to You my Lord. It has been really hot. The weather and the fact that we were in the ocean for two weeks made us edgy. You were there among us. I felt Your presence. It made me smile. Calm seas, winding roads through forest green mountains, suspended bridges, houses built with the skill of an artist, and in the middle is a culture. The culture is reserved, modest, humble, smiling, and colorful. I am on my way to making a phone call to my family and my soulmate. You have placed me today through Your glory and grace in a place on the other side of the world. A place where it is a day earlier and when the sun is going down it is rising in Japan. I went to a baseball game. The Japanese are very nice enthusiastic people. The land and houses are amazing. A bow, a wave, and a smile, the only language that speaks every language. I praise You for arranging Canton and I to explore this fine land. I give all my heart and praises to You the Most High for speaking through our conversation about You.

    Glory to God! I pray that You bless him and his family and answer their prayers. I thank You for introducing me to my brothers and sisters through You at church. I pray that You bless their hearts.

August 25, 2002 (Lincoln Letters)

The blessings never stop and the faith grows stronger. A wise lady told me that I have to look at the earthly things of this world as only being temporary and that Life through the spirit is eternal. Today Canton and I were sitting in a bookstore in Hong Kong. While we were there, Canton asked the manger where the Koran was, and I asked her where the Bible was. Canton made a joke saying we were good friends with two different religions. She said she never heard of that. She said she was a Christian. I started to talk to her about You, my Lord. It turns out Your spirit was speaking to her and through her. I pray that You bless her marriage.

She said Your children are seventeen thousand strong in Hong Kong. Wow, I have seventeen thousand brothers and sisters in China. You are truly amazing, Father. Two people from the opposite sides of the world with the same faith through You. I gave her names to pray for, and she gave me names to pray for. Lord, I pray that You bless all those names and that You send millions of angels to look over them, protect them, and keep them close to You. Keep them close to Your Word. Your Word gave life to us before and after birth.

Lord, I give praises and thanks to You for giving me the blessing of being able to talk to Megan last night. Every time I hear her voice, I feel Your spirit. In our berthing there was a different kind of spirit. An evil one that brought drunken chaos. Our berthing needs more of Your spirit. I pray that your glory, strength, and honor will shine and touch everything in our berthing.

In Jesus's name, I pray. Amen.

September 2, 2002 (Lincoln Letters)

I'm now on my way to visiting You at Your holy house. I pray that You are there among us. We were trying to get to church, and some people were trying to take us there for one hundred dollars. We talked them down to eighty dollars for a closer church that we didn't even know about. Just then, You provided as usual. There was a girl going to the same church we wanted to go to. We are on a free bus with her now going to worship You. I praise You for being among us, for being good to us, and providing us with a way to be closer to You.

Singapore is beautiful. There is a lush forest around the road, overhanging trees, flowers everywhere, and Miami-style buildings. It is really pretty here. There are palm trees everywhere. The church we went to was the City Harvest Church. It is four stories high.

It was so modern on the inside and out that it looked futuristic. I have never seen that many people come to worship You. You are the all mighty God of all creation. The church started with twenty people. It's now up to seven thousand. Your spirit was so powerful. Praise Jesus! The inside looks like it could be the Museum of Modern Art.

Lord, I thank You for providing a beautiful night for this tour. It was raining the whole morning and during the afternoon. I'm on my way to a night safari. It is a four-hundred-acre land of rainforest. I pray that You bless this tour and the ones that find their way into my heart. All praises to the Most High.

September 7, 2002 (Lincoln Letters)

Lord my Father,
    We are entering the Arabian Sea. I feel a seriousness, a vibe that settles beneath the smiles and jokes. The jets that we send up will be loaded with bombs. When they come back, they will be empty. Lord, I pray with all my heart that the things that we do are the will of You, my Lord. You are my gracious Father. I pray that what we do is right by You, Lord. I praise You and need You in the next three months. I feel You each day. At this moment, I'm not sure we will make it back.
    You have placed a strength in my heart. One that releases all fears of death, because death is life. I pray that You send angels around this ship to pull in the direction of Your will and protect us, I pray that You send angels to protect my family, Megan, and friends. I love You, and good night my precious Father.

Dear wonderful Jesus,
    I thank and praise You for the hardships I face on this walk with You. When I see the devil trying to work on me, I can smile and leap for persecution, because the only reason he is trying so hard is because You are bringing me closer to You. I love You, Lord. I yearn for You, precious Father. The further I fall, the harder I reach. The words that You teach is the milk that brings life to the newborn child. I need You, I love You, and I praise You. Without You, I'm nothing.

Father God,
    I thank You for blessing me with so many brothers in You. I pray that Your love, grace, and beautiful spirit will consume Megan from head to toe. Our relationship is an everlasting blessing. I pray that Your guidance in our relationship will be everlasting. I love You, Lord.

October 9, 2002 (Lincoln Letters)

We have been out to sea for around a month. Our mission is sending F-18's, F-14's, E2-C's and S-2's to fly around the region of Afghanistan. We are supporting the ground troops. No bombs have been dropped except two Vikings had to diffuse some of their bombs and drop them (they didn't go off), so they could make it back to the carrier. Words from the XO (Executive Officer). I know You know if those words are true or not, Heavenly Father. I thank You for Your protection, and I pray that You keep sending Your protection and blessings upon this ship.

There are chains that bind us to this earth. These chains could be drugs, alcohol, money, and lust. When these chains become broken to no longer tie us to this earth, we become no longer of this earth. We ascend, we take flight, we elevate. Each elevation brings us closer to our home. The home where we were created. The home, heaven. Our creator, our loving God Himself. The God of creation and the Most High.

I love You, Father. The things of this world are the gravity that keeps us bound to this world. You, my Lord, are everywhere to uplift us. I praise You for Your uplifting spirit, that Your very own Son sacrificed His own life to provide us with. I love You, oh Lord Jesus.

Dear Father God,

I'm truly blessed to have the fresh air in my lungs, the health You have given me. I pray that You place Your healing hands on the sick, so they will realize where glory comes from. It comes from You, Father. I'm completely blessed to have a wonderful family, godly friends, a lovely godly girlfriend, and a Father as awesome as You. You wait for Your children with open, loving, caring arms.

Letters in Vessels

October 11, 2002 (Lincoln Letters)

I fasted for You. I'm not sure if I broke my fast too early. I pray that You guide me to know when you want me to fast again. That You provide me with clarity to know when to break. During my fast, You fed me with the spirit. When my focus was on You, my stomach was filled with Your spirit. The experience humbled me to think less of myself and more of what You do and who You are. I love You, I praise You; I worship You.

October 25, 2002 (Lincoln Letters)

Dear Heavenly Father,
Last Sunday, I fasted for the second time. My fast was a little smoother than the last time. I believe that Your spirit led me to break my fast at the proper time, because when I broke, Your spirit filled me from head to toe. Before I broke, I felt weak and grumpy. Lord, Your presence consumed me and fed me through my fast. I give You thanks and praise for what You have shown me. I prayed that spiritual blindness would be given the eyes to see how much love You have for us all. I prayed for some things that You guided me to pray for. These prayers were for You, my Lord. I pray that You place Your precious hand upon them.

December 6, 2002 (Lincoln Letters)

Oh, gracious, loving, sweet Jesus Christ,

Your love for me is eternal. I'm truly thankful that at times You reside in my soul. I ask You to bless me with a pure walk for the rest of my life on this earth, so Your loving name will be glorified through this unworthy vessel. I ask You for clarity, wisdom, strength, and love, so I can share this salvation You shared with me. It has been around a month since I last wrote to You. Master, as you know, we have been out to sea for this time.

You have been with us the whole time. My soul leaps with joy just to know of Your commitment to all of Your family. During this time, I have heard that our F-18's and F-14's have bombed around twenty-four military sightings. I pray that these sightings were touched with Your hand of protection. I pray that all we do is through Your will and not our own. I will read Your Word now, blessed Master. I ask of You through devotion and prayer that Your glory is seen and felt by everyone in this earth. In Jesus's name I pray, Amen.

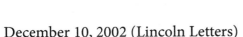

December 10, 2002 (Lincoln Letters)

I'm now in Bahrain with John-o, June, and David. All brothers that You have shined Your grace upon. I thank You for the blessing of being around them. There are times I feel that You send angels on this earth to cross our paths at the specific times You want us to hear Your message. I thank You; I praise You; and I love You, Jesus.

December 11, 2002 (Lincoln letters)

The ones in the states who choose not to accept You into their hearts usually say the reason they don't is because they feel You

Letters in Vessels

have been forced upon them. Thousands of miles away, in Bahrain, a small island next to Saudi Arabia, there's a people who are hungry and thirsty for a salvation that flows through You, my precious Lord. Your message and Your Word are twisted and withheld from them. The authorities rule through religion, not individual rights.

Gracious God,
　I pray for Your precious Son, who leads us in every way. Last night and tonight we crossed paths with a man by the name of Nice.

Loving Jesus,
　You're calling him. I thank You for the opportunity to speak to him of Your grace, peace, salvation, and the love that You have. I pray that the words that we spoke were Your words. I thank You for my precious brothers who prayed with him. He said that we will always be in his heart, just as he will always be in our hearts. I will never forget the light You have placed in his eyes and the wisdom that You have blessed him with.

Oh, gracious Lord,
　As he spoke and accepted You into his heart, the seeds that were planted in his heart will be watered and nourished by You, my Lord. I pray that his roots grow deep in the heart of Your righteousness. Place Your hand of protection over him, my Lord. Give him the answers he seeks for and knowledge to understand those answers. Now he has accepted You, my Lord, grow within him, bless him, and rain Your love upon him. Amen.

December 22, 2002 (Lincoln Letters)

Gracious loving Father,

I praise You. You are the Most High, You reign the heavens and the earth with Your righteousness. We were standing in a long line on the ship. I went to the bathroom. When I came back, I found out that we got head of the line privileges because of Your work through Andy. The XO walked by, and Andy helped him pick up cans. He saw Your grace and glory flowing through Andy. His favor upon us was favor upon You, my Lord. I pray that You show him favor with Your blessings and protection. In Jesus's name I pray, Amen.

December 23, 2002 (Lincoln Letters)

Your love fills me. Waves of grace travel from my head to toe. These waves consume me. The effects are a warm heart. There is no harmony in the midst of discord, my loving Lord. I thank You for my salvation and Your everlasting love for me. It is five-thirty in the morning, and I am in Australia amongst my loving brothers. Saving my soul from death and uniting me with Your body. Gracious loving Lord, I praise You, I worship You, and I thank You. I'm completely blessed to be where I'm at and whom I'm with. Lord, bless my friends and touch them with Your gentle loving hand. Pour out Your grace and glory upon our adventure. In Your loving name I pray, Amen.

You touch me and just from Your finger light fills my body. I feel light. I no longer feel bonded to my own selfish desires. I'm bonded to You and Your desires. Lead me Lord, teach me Lord, love me Lord, show me Your loving way, Jesus. You elevate me and now I see with new eyes. I feel with new hands. I love with my new heart. All glory and grace to You, God. All glory and grace to You, Jesus.

Letters in Vessels

Perth, Australia

Beautiful quaint town, friendly people, evergreens, and old-style buildings. I praise You, Lord. I was walking with the shield of Your Word in my hand. An Aussie started to point toward my hand. He had a huge smile on his face and light shining from his eyes. That light was You, my Lord. It turns out he was pointing at the Bible in my hand. He said, "I see you got your shield." He has been a Christian for eighteen years. Bless him, protect him, supply him with knowledge, strength, and peace. All glory to the Most High of Heaven and Earth. I thank and praise You. In Your loving name I pray, Amen.

I'm on a beautiful beach in Australia. A crisp, clear, sunny and gentle breeze day. Your love is inside of me, Lord. So is Meg's, but I'm missing something. She is not here in the flesh. I can't hug her or talk to her. I know that I desire things of the flesh, but I miss the warmth of Megan's hugs. I also know that even though I'm at least a thousand miles away from Meg, You can bond us as if we were standing right next to each other.

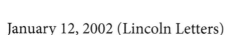

January 12, 2002 (Lincoln Letters)

Third day in Perth, Australia, second time around.

All grace, glory, and peace live inside of You, my loving Jesus. I praise You, sweet Lord for taking favor in me. You have blessed me with open eyes. I praise You, Lord, and I thank You for this clarity. I notice that the devil comes upon me only when I'm weak. Oh, my loving King of kings, I ask for Your strength to follow in your suffering. After knowing what You have showed me, I want to show the world. Sometimes I feel like the world doesn't want to see You, my loving Lord. Your spirit is the great comforter. Comfort this world

Lincoln Letters

with Your spirit, my Lord. Thank You, Jesus, for every day is a new day to live in You.

Your presence magnifies everything. Your touch sends me soaring. I dedicate my life to You, Lord. I'm in Your hands, sweet loving master. I pray for your direction, guidance, wisdom, love, and strength, so that I may have chance to bring glory to Your loving name. In Your loving name I pray, Amen.

The only blood that has fallen upon Your hands was Your own, my precious Jesus. When I live in You, my Lord, You live in me. All glory to the lover of my soul.

January 16, 2002 (Lincoln Letters)

Loving Lord,

Your grace, love, and protection have been upon me in Australia. I have been surfing a lot amongst heavy waves, large sharks, and reefs. I thank You for your hand of protection. I love You, Lord! All glory and honor upon Your name, loving master.

Australia is a beautiful country with friendly people. There is a pub on every corner. The land is amazing. Cliffs, old brick buildings, extremely bright and sunny, evergreen trees, and beautiful crystal-clear beaches. I thank You, Lord, for the works of Your hands.

January 17, 2002 (Lincoln Letters)

It's a beautiful day. Bless Thomas, my Lord. All glory and grace rests in You, my gracious, kind, loving, sweet Jesus. Thank You for putting Your touch upon my spirit. You are burning inside of me ever since You baptized me with Your spirit and fire. Thank You, sweet Lord. Last night, Jesse and I were walking to the train station. All of a sudden, we noticed a plastic bag floating from the sky. It was descending and waving in Your wind upon us. We were drawn to it.

When it got close enough, Jesse snatched it out of the sky. There were two kids sitting on a bench next to this blessed situation. One of the guys asked, "Did that bag just fly out of the sky?"

We said, "Yes."

He said, "That's trippy." We noticed that he had an American accent. We asked where he was from and he said, "Seattle." He said that he and his buddy were doing missionary work. We asked if they were Christian. Their "yes," sparked a reunion of brothers united in You, Jesus.

Tonight, June and I went to a fellowship they invited us to, and it was straight fire in You, Jesus. Bless Josh, Tim, and, Luke. I thank You and give you praise, my awesome Lord, for the connection of us in Your body. Bless them with their studies. Lead them in You and best of all, show them the grace, love, growth, and light that is in You, my Lord.

February 24, 2003 (Lincoln Letters)

Oh, sweet loving Savior. There are days that I feel You have led me astray and have stood aside when I fell, walked away.

Then You enlighten me with a revelation such as this.

When I was a child, my mother put me in a pool where my feet wouldn't touch, and she would walk out of reach. I would panic with the insecurity of knowing she wasn't there to keep my head above the water. I would kick my feet and wave my arms, try my hardest to get within her grasp. Just when my head started to go under, she would come to my rescue and lift me up. It turns out that as I was panicking and longing to be within her reach, I was learning how to swim to her instead of her walking to me.

Jesus Christ (the visible God)

God is spirit. Spirit cannot be seen or felt unless that spirit reveals Himself to the senses. Jesus Christ is God revealing himself to our senses. God stirs the wind. Jesus is the movement of that tree which lets us know that the wind exists. Without being able to touch, smell, taste, hear, or see Him, how can we know God exists? Without feeling the sensation of God, we don't and never will know God. Jesus Christ is the one who brings that sensation.

April 23, 2003 (Lincoln Letters)

It has been two months since I have written to You, my loving Savior of grace. I bless Your name, my Lord. You have brought me through so much in so little time. You have blessed me with unexpected favor that could only come from You. I work in the tower now with V-5. Thank You for Your blessings and Your sufferings. We have been through a war during this time. The first day we started bombing, You let me feel a small portion of the anguish felt by both sides. You have spread the fellowship of this ship to different parts of the world.

June, Andy, Bobby, and other brothers and sisters have been spread to plant seed on different ground. Every night You have brought the message of life to this ship. Each night we hear of a child being born back home. Bless and protect them, Lord. We have been on deployment for nine months; we haven't seen land for three months—almost a hundred days—and all I can feel is the complete joy of being a Christian.

When you give up everything, you gain everything you realized you never had. I love You so much, my beautiful Lord and Savior. I have been struggling in my walk with You, my Lord. I have not been digesting and meditating on Your Word like I should be doing. When I don't invite You in, I find myself longing for Your presence. I praise You and thank You for the longing you place in my heart. I need You when I fall. I need You when I sleep.

I need You when I wake. I need You always. These temptations, the distant glances of lost souls, the suffering, the persecutions, the hardened hearts that nail You to the cross through disbelief, the void that cannot be filled with excess or pleasures of this world. In fact, that void expands when fulfilling those pleasures.

The empty conversations that break instead of build. The eyes that are scared to look into other eyes by the fear of what these eyes might see. All of these sorrows that are revealed to me kill me, and they are only a grain of sand in the seashore of sorrow you suffer through Jesus. Through it all, there is peace in my heart and an immense love that You have sowed within my soul. This is only found in You.

I thank You, Jesus, for opening my eyes to see how much You love every person in this world. I pray for every person that You put in my path. I ask for strength to walk in Your love. I pray that Your Word, which You have placed within me, will come out when my faith is tried and tested. Touch every heart, my Lord. Lift the burdens off heavy hearts. Cover this world in Your blood. Your blood cleanses, washes us clean, purifies us, and was spilt out of Your precious body so that through Your death and resurrection, we would be saved. Thank You, Jesus. Thank You for pulling me out of death.

On a wheel, the potter places a lump of clay lying shapeless, cold, and parched from the sun. Cracks, lines, and wrinkles stretch around its surface, with only a remembrance of the water it was snatched out of. The springs that sustained its life and the hands that placed it there. The potter looks upon the wheel at the clay.

The clay is rough, lowly, and the parched scars lie beneath its surface. The potter dips his cradled hands into a beautifully shaped pot and fetches out life-giving water. The water drips through the cracks between the potter's fingers and drops onto the clay, bringing everything to life it touches. All the scars blend and fade. At this moment, there is a breaking down. The pot is humbled back down to the wheel. The wheel spins the pot to dizziness. Those reassuring comforting hands begin to shape the pot.

With a sound of the trumpet warned before the fall of the sword. Your foot strikes the sky and pierces the clouds. Oh, Most High, Your glory reigns in this watchful eye. I wait for Your love to fill the earth, and I wait for every knee to bow. Lord, I thank You for allowing me to sing to You in the midst of flesh and sin. I thank You that You purge the dross, my Lord. I ask for Your strength to be magnified within me.

Lord, I want to live for You. I pray that this pride, this self-righteousness (not one is righteous but You), apathy, lack of patience, selfishness, anger, complacency, lust, fear, and idleness will die within me. I pray that it will go into the grave and never come out. Lord, I want Your life, love, and spirit to take its place. Please forgive me, Lord. Living for me stops me from living for You. I want to die for You, so I can live within You. Take over. I give You the driver's wheel. I get lost all of the time, usually driving in circles. You see and know everything. I want to follow Your direction. Lord, please take my hand and lead me down Your strait. I want to know You more and more.

> "He is no fool, who gives up what he cannot keep to gain what he cannot lose." ([4]Benge, One Great Purpose, Synopsis.)

Letters in Vessels

Sometime during April and May 2003 (End of deployment)
(Lincoln Letters)

Through the process of growing, things take place that I don't really understand until the process is over.

(A conversation with a friend)

Question: If you had a friend who was about to drive off a cliff, knew what was on the other side of the cliff, tried to warn him and he kept driving, how would that make you feel?
Answer: Not good.
Question: What would you do?
Answer: Keep warning him?
Question: What if he kept driving?
Answer: Keep trying, don't give up?

This was the last entry I made during my first deployment (July 2002–May 2003) in support of Operation Iraqi Freedom (Lincoln Letters).

During the first week back from deployment, I proposed to Megan. In Washington, there is a season when they grow fields of tulips. It is amazing. There are fields of tulips as far as the eye can see. I tried to take Megan to one of those fields to propose. The only problem was they already harvested the fields, and I could not find one field to propose in. I was freaking out.

I was driving everywhere looking for a field and Megan was wondering why I was so caught up in tulips. I pulled over on the side of the rode in a parking lot. I noticed a dirt path in the woods. Megan and I walked down that path. I had no clue what I was going to do then suddenly the path opened up to a beautiful lake with mountains in the background. I took advantage of the opportunity and proposed.

Letter from Megan about the proposal
May 13, 2003

Today, Anthony proposed to me! We were in Washington. He took me out beside a lake. We were looking out at the lake and the mountains. It was beautiful. Then he turned to me. My heart dropped. He said, "Meg, I love you with all my heart" then he hit one knee and said, "Megan, I love you and I want to spend the rest of my life with you. Will you marry me?" I said yes, and he put the ring on my finger.

We had our wedding on August 30, 2003, and it was official. We were Mr. and Mrs. Diamandi. Those moments are and always will be the best moments of my life.

Dear God,

This seems like the best way of comunication for myself. Writing that is. I know you know this. I would like to Apologize for putting my prayers on paper. I know my head is down while I write to you; however, I will finish these prayers to you with my head up and reading them back to you silently. I believe that you are extremely compassionate and you are willing to accept all of us as we are as long as we come to you with our hearts open. I come to you today in this prayer with my heart open and my hand reaching for yours. I'm knocking on your door. I pray you give me the guidance to look after everything to my best ability. I notice your work every time I see a sunset, the ocean, stars, Megan, Ashley, Mom, Dad, Grandy Nanny, Oeda, Mema, Papa, Lee, Tia Lynn, Rachel, A kind sole, Monica, Kelly Kristen, Tia Ruby, uncle Billy, and so on. I admire your work. It is beutful and Majestic.

1st Letter

Megan and Tony Diamandi

11

Held Up in Prayer

Second Deployment October 2004–March 2005
Deployment during Banda Aceh tsunami and flood. (Lincoln Letters)

Lord,
Give me the courage to not give up. I ask for Your strength to be able to press toward the mark, to have pleasure and joy through the fellowship of Your sufferings. To live Your same love that redeemed the world. I ask to be able to look toward Your guidance and to walk in it with a faith that will not question. In Your glorious name, I ask these things according to Your will. In Jesus's name I pray, Amen.

There once was a man who loved God with his whole heart. He loved God so much that he carried his Lord inside of him. The Lord loved the man back. So much, that the Lord's love flowed from the inner man to the outside world. The world around the man hated God. Not because God wasn't good. It was because when God was around, the world's intentions and actions which were against God would be revealed. The man who loved God was also hated by the world, because he carried his Lord inside of him. They would cut this man with the very words that they would speak.

Each word would tear the flesh right off the man's bones. The tearing would be extremely painful. A ripping, stinging pain that would demand all attention from the man going through it. During this process something amazing was taking place, a miracle. While the flesh was being stripped away through persecution, his Lord beneath his flesh was being seen even more. His flesh which was covering his Lord was being peeled away and now uncovering his Lord for the world to see, until this man didn't even look like a man anymore. Instead, he looked like his God who was magnified inside of him.

Take a small cup. Place it in a jar. If you keep pouring water, it will flow out of the cup and into the jar. So much that the cup will no longer hold the water. Instead, the water will hold the cup submerged beneath its surface. The water will drown the cup. Take a small cup, place several cups around it. This time, when the water reaches the brim, pour it into the next cup and so on until the last one is filled. Keep the water flowing and the process going until all the cups are full. We are empty vessels. God's blessings are continuously flowing. If we try to store all His blessings for ourselves, the blessings will overflow the brim. We will be focused on the blessing.

The blessing will be in control of us if we live holy as the Father is holy and bless others, pouring out the blessing within us to fill them, teaching them to do the same. All are filled with the blessings of the almighty God, which are continuously flowing.

John 11 (Jesus raises Lazarus from the dead.)

Lord,

You waited two days after hearing of Lazarus's sickness before you journeyed to him. During this time, he died. You knew that Your glory would be revealed (John 11:15) by raising him from the dead. Did You wait because of Your compassion for Mary, Martha, and the Jews would have compelled you to heal him before he died?

John 11:35: "Jesus wept." Lord, You suffer at the sight of our suffering. It moves You to action. You raised Lazarus from the dead. Mary, Martha, and the Jews didn't believe that You were the resurrection and the life. They heard it, but had never seen it. They had faith that You could keep him alive. Their faith was about to grow by seeing him raised from the dead.

My Lord,

I ask for Your ability to love as You love, Lord. To have a new heart within me that would be so moved with compassion for those around me that I can feel as they feel, just as You did. I ask that You use me to help and be able to discern those who really want to know You and don't know how to search You out. Help me point the way to You. I pray that You send the hungry my way. I pray that your spirit will guide me in what to say, when to say it, and who to say it to. I bless You, Lord, and I thank You that You are life. In Jesus's name I pray. Amen.

Lord of Life,

I thank You and praise Your most holy name for all life. Everything that has breath grows, lives, was created, and is sustained through You. I bless Your name, my Lord. Fill this world, Your creation, with Your glory. The very spirit that descended upon You in the shape of a dove while our Father, who only by You can we be adopted as sons, said, "This is my beloved son whom I am well pleased." Lord, I pray as You pray; may Your kingdom be established on Earth. I thank You for Your presence in my life. When You explained to the disciples how all the prophets in the Scriptures pointed to You, their hearts were warm inside. Thank You, Master, for breathing Your life spirit into my heart. I thank You for Your presence in all hearts who the Father has opened for You. You are so amazing, my Lord. I praise You, bless You, and give You thanks for Your love. A love that has no thought of one's self.

Lord,

You poured out Your life to all who were around You, and You still do. Not one part of You was selfish. I want to live like that.

You are my personal Savior and Savior of the world. I love You, Lord, and ask that You manifest Your presence in my life and those around me on this day.

My Lord,

You search us out. Not because You have to. You want to. You have no need of us, yet we have complete need of You.

"Since he is the being supreme over all. It follows that God cannot be elevated. Nothing is above him nothing is beyond him. Any motion in his direction is elevation for the creature; away from him, descent." ([5]Tozer, The Knowledge of The Holy, 33.)

Lord,

I saw You with Your arms open wide. I went up to hug You, and instead of hugging me back, You accepted me inside of You. In You, my arms are opened wide accepting the next person into Your body.

When I open Your Word or look into the eyes of someone who is allowed to know what You have allowed me to know. When I close my eyes and speak to You, I'm lifted out of the cold steel. You remind me that wherever I go, You are with me. When I'm lifted into Your heart, there is no place I would rather be. I'm completely free in You. You lift me into Your kingdom which is You. There are no limits to Your grace and goodness. I bless You, Father, for Your perfect way for me to meet Your precious Son, Jesus Christ. I love You, Jesus! You are blessed eternally. Glory unto You. You fill the world with Your presence.

I'm forever thankful. Your wisdom guides us and leads us to perfection. In You, there is no blemish. The just testify in one smile. You surround Your chosen with favor and grace. You are a mighty tower for the afflicted. Continue to turn hearts to seek You and to read Your covenants, promises that will never be broken. Your Word will last forever. Your Word is the rock of our foundation. I bless You, Lord. I love You. I thank You. You are the Most High living God.

Vision:

It always seems like the middle of the night. The fourth watch. No one is around but You and me. I can see You. My vision is clouded. I can't see you for who You completely are, just a glimpse of You. A glimpse of Your shadow overtakes me. I want to get as close as I can to You. I start to walk toward You. You walk forward, creating a bigger gap between us. This gap makes me feel empty inside because I have had the taste of Your presence. In frustration, I wear myself out trying to get close to You. With compassion, You wait, filling me with Your presence, taking my breath away, filling me with bliss.

You restore me. You walk again. You turn a corner. Where did You go? I feel lost when I can't see You. I get to the corner. Where did You go? I feel lost when I can't see You. I get to another corner. I see You again. I have never caught up to You or seen You in full clarity. You have always led me to move forward, toward You. I think the reason I never catch You or why I can't clearly see You is because You haven't called me home yet.

> 1 Corinthians 13:9-12 (NKJV):
> For we know in part and we prophesy in part. But when that which is perfect has come, then that which is in part will be done away. When I was a child, I spoke as a child, I understood as a child, I thought as a child, but when I became a man, I put away childish things. For now, we see in a mirror dimly, but then face to face, now I know in part, but then I shall know just as I also am known.

A child loves its parents. The moment that child's mother or father walks out of its reach, that child feels helpless. That child clings to its parents. If that child could be one hundred percent a part of its parents' life, he or she is all for it. That child starts to grow up.

All of a sudden, its parents aren't as cool as they used to be. The child is more interested in going with what he or she doesn't know rather than its parent who gave that child everything, including themselves. That parent waits. The child will eventually come back. I'm the child, Father. God, You are the parent. Thank You for waiting and willing me back.

Lord,

Here I am, sin all around me. Sin trying to rise up inside of me. I worship You, Lord. I know what You are about to do. Well, only a portion because You will do more than I can imagine. My Lord, it seems like wickedness and evil are flooding this world and trying to claw at Your saints' feet, pulling us out of your hands. I know Your hands, strong and powerful. At the power of Your right hand, all evil will not only fall before your feet, but also my feet. I know You can see these attacks on my wife from Satan, the fallen angel.

You have revealed it to me. I thank You for bringing the darkness to light. What is done in darkness will always be brought to light. I thank You for Your protection in the midst of the valley. Lord, You comfort me. I know You are with me. Your spirit confirms Your presence. Everything I have in this world will pass away. I surrender all that I have to You, because I know You are all I need.

Wickedness can only take what I have already surrendered. This battle that comes against Your saints, You fight. You have already won, Lord Jesus. You have already defeated all principalities and powers at the cross. Lord, Your day is coming when every knee shall bow. Every word that has been spoken will be revealed.

You give me Your strength to patiently wait for that glorious day. Bless, protect, and fill Megan's heart with as much of You as she can take. Let Your grace be her pillow. I pray she can rest her head on Your grace. Fill her with Your joy and love, my Lord. In the name of Your Son, Jesus Christ, our Messiah, Amen.

I wake up with oppression, captivity, chains, and shackles around me. You are with me. You stand in Your glory. Arms spread out, stretched as wings. You motion them to You. With every motion a new man walks into Your presence. Shackles fall to the ground. Chains shatter to pieces. No more walls, no more gates, no more bars, no more locks. Freedom in a sky with no ground beneath with no limits, endless and eternal. You step into a room, it changes. When the light of new day arises on the earth, the shadows run.

They hide beneath trees. Lord, You turn the shadows into shade. When You shelter a man with Your presence, he can walk in the rain and not get wet. A beautiful woman stands firm, face glowing with the radiance of a love that only a child could have. Pure love. Her hands are raised in praise.

She is standing in this world, but her heart is in the kingdom of heaven. As she praises You, a light fills a body that cannot contain it. Lord, Your light shoots out of her in every direction. Demons, dark spirits surround her, posed as bulls. Their front right foot striking the ground, ready to charge. Running full charge, directly toward her with intentions of ripping her to pieces. She stands firm, perfect praise. She doesn't even notice them.

Her eyes are focused on our King. The bulls run toward her. As they get close, they have to run in the opposite direction. They turn away from the light, away from my wife. Some get too close to the light. They turn to nothing; they evaporate. In the center, there is a glow where all the darkness flees or is consumed by the light.

What is my expectation of Jesus?

I expect You to love me, to never leave me nor forsake me. To always be faithful in Your Word. To never lie and to draw all men toward You. I expect that when I'm with You, I will need nothing else.

There has been a lot of things happening on the Lincoln. A man got his leg run over by a jet that was being towed (leg remained intact). A woman got hit in the head by the wing of a jet that was being launched off the catapult (she survived). The latest, a helicopter crash (all survived). Just like the helicopter, the body is all beat up, but the center, the soul, is untouched. All have lived.

Why? An earthquake happens right next to us. Hundreds of thousands of people die, we're still alive. Why? I think the prayers of Your saints are sparing us. As this wickedness increases, the saints are no longer praying for the wicked to be protected. They are now praying for their own protection against the wicked.

> Exodus 14:14 (NKJV)
> "The Lord will fight for you and you shall hold your peace."

It starts with ten people (the bride). They are walking to the bridegroom. They are being led by the spirit. As the spirit leads the bride, ten turns into fifty; fifty turns into five hundred; five hundred into a thousand, until no man can count the bride being led by the spirit to the bridegroom.

I can feel Your pursuit. I turn and look into Your eyes. Eyes of consuming passion and love. The look within Your eyes burns inside of me. I want to be as close as I can to You. My heart flutters, and I pant for Your warmth. I feel secure in Your arms. When You speak, I come to life. I love You. I long to be with You, rest my head on Your chest, listen to the beat of Your heart, to hear the rhythm that holds all existence together. Your heart beats for me, flowing with a love as pure as You without blemish and clear as crystal.

I never want to leave Your side. Can I tag along forever? Better yet, can I dive inside of You? Fly inside of Your endless atmosphere. I find healing in Your wings.

Thank you, Father (Daddy).

I thank You for speaking through Tim today. I know You were speaking. It is not about what I know or how I am or what I do. It always comes down to You, my loving Father who loves always, always has loved, and will love me through it all. I thank You, Dad. I know it has taking me a long time to say that with the feelings I feel now. I know You know all things. I love You, Daddy. I want to wait to run into your arms after You have had a long day in the office.

I want to share my day with You, hear You laugh, smell Your smell, fall asleep in Your arms. Thank You for loving me, Dad. Just when I feel scared, overwhelmed, and tired, You scoop me up. You hold me close. You speak, and the world stops. It's just me and You. I love You, Daddy.

Me and You, once again, in the middle of the night. I couldn't sleep, Lord. The guys I work with are on my heart. I feel like within my heart I want to wake them up out of a bad dream. It seems like they are so used to that bad dream they don't want to wake up. It is all they know. I know within there is a sadness. It makes me sad.

A void that is empty that can only be filled by You. Lord, if only they knew the freedom You are, not bondage. I feel like everything within me is screaming to deaf ears. I end up not even speaking. You are the Father of comfort. Thank You for comforting me. Thank You! I know it breaks Your heart. You love with an endless love for people who only call You when we feel we need You. Remind me to be thankful always.

To realize that no matter what I do or where I go You follow me. You love me regardless. You call me Your son. Open the eyes of my friends, so they can see what I see in You. There is nothing bad in You. All things good: purity, love, peace, patience, truth, and strength. You take a slap in the face and give back a hug. That is so awesome. I want to be like that. The person You have created me to be wants to show them a love so pure. A love that would die for his friends and his brothers.

Lord, take my friends back to the cross. The same cross You hung on, pouring Your life out, losing Your blood, going through a pain that not one person could say they have felt. You have done this for every person, so they could overcome death and walk into eternal life through You. I love You and ask that You lead them to Your love. In Jesus's glorious name I pray, Amen.

I love You, Jesus.

Lord,

Just as Josh said, I feel it also. I feel dull. My devotion to You is being distracted by what's around me. Lord, as I draw close to You, I know You draw close to me. Draw close. I call for Your presence. I don't know what to do without You. In You, there is peace. I pray that I will not focus on me, but rather focus on You. I pray that every distraction and disillusion that tries to separate Your children from each other and You will have no power. Unite us, my Lord! Take off our ways, the ways of man. I bless You, Jesus. I love You. I want You to be where my heart is found. I know what You begin, You will finish. You will perfect it. I trust in You! Thank You! I love You!

Jesus: The heart of God given to us from the Father.

Holy Spirit: The heart of Jesus given to us from the Son.

They are all one.

During the editing part of this book, there came a point where I had to cite references. I knew from the start of this process that there would be three letters which would have to be treated differently, with reverence and prayer. I would have to take this to the one who was in this from the beginning and will see it to the end. I would have to take it to God.

When those three letters were written, I did not look up the words in the Bible. I did not write them from memory. I am not wise or tedious enough in my studies to memorize all the words that were spoken in those letters. I cannot cite King James, New Living, Message or New International Versions for those letters. The only one I can cite is God spoken through His Holy Spirit. I know that not everyone who reads this will understand what I am saying. They will want me to point to something they can physically see or go to. A book of some sort, a source. If God spoke to His loved ones in the past, why would he stop speaking to His loved ones now and in the future?

The true source is not just found in the pages of a book. His Spirit is everywhere. He was found on the nights when I was reaching out to Him through those letters. He spoke and I wrote it down. It is all Him. He is my citing He is my source. He is the whole reason why I am writing right now. My existence and all I do is found in Him and His love.

If the verses are needed, I have done the research and found the verses which match what was spoken to me over a decade ago by the Holy Spirit. If you question it, look it up. Look into the Bible and look at history to see if what was spoken came to pass. I have put alphabetical superscripts in those letters. The reason I have used the superscripts separately from the verses is to not disrupt the flow of what is being said. The verses can be found in the Bibliography next to the same superscripts.

Letter 1 of 3

Lord,

You comfort me with Your love. No matter what it looks like in front of my eyes, You are inside of me. I can feel You, Jesus. Thank

Letters in Vessels

You for your breath, the Holy Spirit. The wind of God. Thank You for Your strength, the rock, my shelter and strong tower. Thank You for Your passion; let it burn within me. I love You, Jesus. Thank You for turning this situation around for good. I know You are faithful. Great Shepherd, who leads us to streams of living water, come move with Your power. Let Your glory be revealed before all eyes, including mine. I bless You, my holy Lord. "I'm going to move. I'm going to tear down strongholds."

"^A The exalted will be abased. ^A The humble will be strengthened. ^B I will take my people from all sides and gather them from all sides. ^C I'm calling you out: come, come. ^A I gather you, my people, from the four winds. ^D I will breathe my breath into your nostrils. ^E You will speak my words. ^F You own the land that you live in. ^F I have given it to you. ^G It is not by your might, but by mine. ^H I go before you. ^I My grace is endless."

"^J I give it to you not as the world gives. Follow me, pick up your cross, hear my words, live in them, and abide them and I will abide in you. ^L I have given you power from above. You have my spirit, I love you, you are my son. ^M I will never forsake you. ^M I will never let you down. ^N I come to give you strength. ^O You have my Son."

"^O I have given Him up as a sacrifice that you might be saved. Believe with all your heart, and I will show you what you have not seen. ^P I come to give you peace to a world that knows no rest. ^Q I am the light and in me is no darkness. Go tell Megan what I have told you. I love you both."

Thank you, Jesus.

Jesus walks up to the Abraham Lincoln. The "shall not perish" banner catches His eye. He says, "I have come that none shall perish and whoever believes in me shall have everlasting life." He walks across the brow. He stops where the sailors salute the Ensign. The fifty states speak out, "We were founded and created through You, we salute You."

The color red speaks out, "I represent the blood of those who have fought and fallen for freedom, but Your blood was spilt to cover the whole world and redeem all men and women who believe that they may be free from sin and death, I salute You."

The color white speaks out, "I stand for purity, but You are the unblemished lamb who did not sin, I salute You."

The color blue speaks out, "I stand for truth, but You are the way the truth and the life, I salute You."

Jesus approaches the ID checker and shows the young man his hand. The young man, with a tear in his eye, says, "Lord, in Your hand is all the ID I need. Your scars show me and everyone on this ship that You were dead and now You are alive and before me, welcome aboard."

The next stop Jesus makes is the mess decks. As he walks through the chow line, He says, "I am the bread of life, the manna from heaven, remember the thousands I fed in the desert with two fish and five loaves of bread. Remember that there were twelve baskets left after everyone was full. Come with me and you will never go hungry again. My food is to do the will of my Father." He passes by the drinks and says, "I have living water; whoever drinks of the water I give will never thirst. For out of his belly shall flow springs of living water." All follow him.

Jesus walks through medical. With a touch of His garment, the sick are made whole. Jesus walks up to the bridge where the captain is, taps him on the shoulder and says, "I am here to take this vessel to my Father."

The captain turns around and says, "You are the path of light who has kept this ship on course, this ship is Yours."

Jesus takes the wheel and steers us into the distant horizon where the kingdom of heaven awaits.

This is one of my last writings on the Lincoln. My time for reenlistment was coming fast. I was not sure if I wanted to reenlist. I prayed about it.

One night, I was on the treadmill when God started showing what He wanted me to do. I got to the end of my run and could feel the Lord wanting me to increase the speed of the treadmill, so I did. This would happen several times. Each time, God would tell me to increase the speed, so I would. Each time God would tell me to increase the speed, I would think it was impossible. In my doubt, I could hear the Lord telling me to trust Him. The speed would go up, and I would find it painful not wanting to do it.

I was running faster and further than I thought I could. Once my time ran out, the Lord wanted me to run at that pace until He told me to start slowing things down, so I did with apprehension. At that moment, the lesson behind this started to sink in. The Lord was showing that He would lead me into places that I did not want to go. That I would kick and scream against it. I would tell the Lord it was too hard, that I would not do it. Out of my love for Him, I would follow Him into the unknown. I already knew that the unknown with Him was far better than the known without Him. The beauty and the reward will overcome the ashes and the cost. He was showing me that I would go places and experience things I never dreamed, so I reenlisted.

Before I reenlisted, I was up for orders and had to pick a billet (place and job that I would be working at for my next reenlistment). During that time, there was a list of jobs and places that were open for the rate I was in. I asked Megan where she wanted to go and getting back to the East Coast was important to her. It was important to me as well. During the first selection, I picked a couple East Coast billets even though they were not on the list. This happened a few times, and each time, I would get denied. The last selection came up real fast. Megan and I had to pick the billets on the list.

I remember reading Megan the choices and she said that she would rather pick Japan then one of the other billets. I took this literally and picked Japan with four other choices. I was at the end of my last deployment on the Lincoln in Hawaii when I received my orders for the next three years in Atsugi, Japan.

I called Megan to tell her, and she said, "Are you serious?" before she hung up on me. I called her three times that day and every time I called, she hung up on me. The only words I got from her that helped me understand why she was hanging up on me was that she did not mean that she wanted Japan literally. She would rather get Japan than the other place, and she could not believe that we were going to live in Japan. It turned out that once we got into Japan, God could not have picked a better match for Megan. The people in Japan are humble, gentle, and friendly, just like Megan. They had amazing skin care, a fashion sense that was up her alley, and she loved the food, not to mention the sights and landscapes.

12

Japan Letters

These entries/letters were not specifically dated, but were written during the three years I spent in my second reenlistment in Japan for shore duty in 2007 to 2010.

Lord,
 I just read today that Paul, his prize, the crown of righteousness, will be given to him when You return. It was just laid up for him at his death. His labor for You is still doing Your work even as I read his letter. He was about to die.

2 Timothy 4:8

 I stand in my way a prisoner of myself and doing what I want instead of what You want me to do. Deep cries out to deep. The part of me that has been touched by You cries out to You for the rest of my body to be set free, released into Your hands. Help me to fully open up to You. You know the things I hide from You anyway. You search me out. You know all my ways, my comings and goings, whether they be physical or spiritual. If there is a problem in my life, it is not a fault with You, my wife, my friends, my family, or my enemies. The problem starts with me. Something is being worked out in me bringing me closer to You. The lower I become, the more I realize how exalted You are.

In a Man

There is a raging war going on full force, guns blazing, loud bangs, screaming, flashing images moving too fast to make any sense of what's going on at the time. Sense is made in retrospect. People are dying and being rescued at the same time. Too much pain for these eyes to see. At the height of calamity, a king comes from heaven. The fighting ceases. The warriors who have become heroes during the battle bow at his feet. The dead are raised, they bow to You also. I can see that the enemy vanished. They seem as an illusion now.

I love You, Jesus (King of kings).

> 1 Corinthians 1:5–7 (NKJV)
> "That you were enriched in everything by Him in all utterance all knowledge, even as the testimony of Christ was confirmed in you, so that you come short in no gift, eagerly waiting for the revelation of our Lord Jesus Christ."

Having a relationship with Almighty God through the ways He provided. We can't just come into Your presence unless You provide a way. You are a consuming fire.

> Exodus 24:17 (NKJV)
> "The sight of the glory of the Lord was like a consuming fire on top of the mountain in the eyes of the children of Israel."

> Exodus 33:20-23 (NKJV):
> But He said, "You cannot see my face; for no man shall see me, and live." And the Lord said, "Here is

a place by me, and you shall stand on the rock. So it shall be, while My glory passes by, that I will put you in the cleft of the rock, and will cover you with my hand while I pass by. Then I will take away My hand and you shall see my back; but My face shall not be seen."

In the beginning, man (Adam) was in direct relationship with God. God planted a garden and put man in it (Gen. 2:8).

He even brought animals to Adam to see what he would name them (Gen. 2:19).

God created Adam a companion (Gen. 2:22).

The relationship is broken when sin is introduced. Adam and Eve were deceived by the serpent. They disobeyed the Lord by eating the fruit He told them not to eat (Gen. 3:6).

They sinned, curses entered into the world, and they were cast out of God's presence in the garden. Cherubim guarded Eden with flaming swords to stop man from entering into the place where direct communion with God was taking place (Gen. 3:24).

Man entered this new world where evil and good were present. One of the examples of this was the first murder. Cain killed Abel. A wickedness began to rule the land (Gen. 6:5-6).

God sent the flood that wiped out all men except Noah and his family (Gen. 6:18-19).

God provided another way into His presence (the tabernacle). Only chosen people (the priest) could enter this place. He had mercy toward man and provided a way back into his presence through commandments (Exod. 25:22).

Lord,

It was like You were saying, "Look, man didn't get this commandment thing down. Maybe we should go over it a little more."

This time, there were cherubim in the tabernacle. Unlike the garden where they had swords out ready to strike anyone who was trying to enter God's presence. They were doing something different in the tabernacle. The wings of the cherubim were covering or overshadowing the cover that was on top of the Ark of the Testimony.

> Exodus 25:22 (NKJV)
> "And there I will meet with you, and I will speak with you from above the mercy seat, from between the two cherubim where are on the ark of the Testimony, about everything which I will give to you in commandment to the children of Israel."

The cherubim were covering the place where God would dwell, and He would give commandments to a chosen priest who would share those commandments with the people. The priest would enter behind a veil and speak with God. The only way for God's people to be right with Him were to obey all of His commandments. If they disobeyed, they would bring a sacrifice to the priest to make atonement for their sins. Only the high priest could go to the most holy place behind the veil.

> Hosea 6:6 (NKJV)
> "For I desired mercy and not sacrifice, and the knowledge of God more than burnt offerings."

Old Testament: Jesus concealed.
New Testament: Jesus revealed.
The veil was torn apart when Jesus was crucified (Matt. 27:51).
All who go through Jesus come into the most holy place and have direct relationship with God (Heb. 10:9–13).
We have been made holy through the sacrifice of Jesus Christ once and for all.

Laughter

"Things never happen the same way twice, dear one" ([6]*Lewis and Neeson, The Chronicles of Narnia/Prince Caspian. DVD.*) You are so beloved that God couldn't stand to let you go. Your little light shined bright in the stars above (the miscarriage). We feel it might have been a girl. Tony would have never been born if it didn't happen.

> Philippians 2:5-11 (NKJV)
> Let this mind be in you which was also in Christ Jesus, who, being in the form of God, did not consider it robbery to be equal with God, but made himself of no reputation, taking the form of a bondservant, and coming in the likeness of men, and being found in appearance as a man, He humbled himself, and became obedient to the point of death, even the death of the cross. Therefore God also has highly exalted Him and given Him the name that is above every name, that at the name of Jesus every knee should bow, of those in heaven, and of those on earth, and of those under earth, and that every tongue should confess that Jesus Christ is Lord, to the glory of God the father.

What the human heart longs for (all mankind longs for these things):

Comfort: To know that everything will be okay. To know that you're so important that someone would do anything for your welfare.

Peace: Deep down everyone really wants not to be in tension. Conflict hurts both sides.

Acceptance: To be yourself and be accepted for who you are. To be welcomed in your most vulnerable state.

Intimacy: To love and be loved.
Joy: To be happy.

All this is found in Him.

The price Jesus paid was not cheap. He gave us His all. His whole life was poured out for us. He gave us Himself. He wants us to give Him everything. This is why we must count the cost. What is amazing is that when we give Him everything, we realize that what we gave You, Lord, was really nothing at all in comparison to what You gave us. We give all that we have, which is nothing, and gain You. All things were created in You, by You, and through You.

Matthew 6:11-21(NKJV)
Do not lay up for yourselves treasures on earth, where moth and rust destroy and where thieves break in and steal; but lay up for yourselves treasures in heaven where moth nor rust destroys and where thieves do not break in and steal. For where your treasure is there your heart will be also.

John 3:1-8 (NKJV)
There was a man of the Pharisees named Nicodemus, a ruler of the Jews. This man came to Jesus by night and said to Him, "Rabbi, we know that You are a teacher come from God; for no one can do these signs that You do unless God is with him." Jesus answered and said to him, "Most assuredly, I say to you, unless one is born again, he cannot see the kingdom of God." Nicodemus said to him, "How can a man be born when he is old? Can he enter a second time into his mother's womb and be born?" Jesus answered, "Most assuredly, I say to you, unless one is born of water and the Spirit, he cannot enter

the kingdom of God. That which is born of the flesh is flesh, and that which is born of Spirit is Spirit. Do not marvel that I said to you, 'you must be born again.' The wind blows where it wishes, and you hear the sound of it, but cannot tell where it comes from and where it goes. So is everyone who is born of the spirit."

Nicodemus answered and said to him, "How can these things be?" Jesus answered and said to him, "Are you the teacher of Israel, and do not know these things? Most assuredly, I say to you, We speak what We know and testify what We have seen, and you do not receive Our witness. If I have told you earthly things and you do not believe, how would you believe if I tell you heavenly things? No one has ascended to heaven but He who came down from heaven, that is, the Son of Man who is in heaven. And as Moses lifted up the serpent in the wilderness, even so must the Son of Man be lifted up, that whoever believes in Him should not perish but have eternal life. For God so loved the world that He gave His only begotten Son, that whoever believes in Him should not perish but have everlasting life. For God did not send His Son into the world to condemn the world, but that the world through Him might be saved. "He who believes in Him is not condemned; but he who does not believe is condemned already because he has not believed in the name of the only begotten Son of God."

13

Two Become Three

Lord,
On April 29, 2009, You gave me a son. You and I both know that it didn't come easy. Once, we (Megan and I) weren't able to conceive. There was a miscarriage along the way; that is how "Laughter" was written. I believe that there are little souls that are so precious in Your sight, Lord, that they stay with You.

I remember that a time after that, Megan showed me the pregnancy tests, which were positive. It was such a blessing. There was a fear about the same thing happening twice, but I remember that after the miscarriage I saw The Chronicles of Narnia. In that movie, the lion, who is You, says, "Things never happen the same way twice, dear one." ([6]Lewis and Neeson. The Chronicles of Narnia/Prince Caspian. DVD.) were preparing me to believe that this time would be different.

Before Megan was pregnant, it was so awesome how You told her that she would have a boy and he was strong and he would make it. You spoke to me, saying to give him the name that had been given to me. At first, I rebelled against the notion, saying my son will never be a third. I remember You telling me to give him that name, that he would be like me and You would give him the spirit of Ezekiel. That is powerful, Lord.

It kind of made sense, because I thought about calling him Tony. I strongly believe that my father came to know You at the end of his earthly life, which I'm sure had an impact on me coming to know you after his death. It says in Your Word that when someone lets You in that their children's children, and I think it even goes to another generation, are open to being blessed in You. It is like Tony, my dad. During a portion of his life, he left a legacy of rebellion, but he made a decision to follow You before he left. You forgave him and gave him a peace that we all could see in the way that he went.

Now, little Tony, my son, can carry out that fellowship with You, my Lord, in his own way, and on this side of the mountain there will be a legacy of love, faith, and a strength attached to this name, Tony Diamandi. That is kind of the way I made sense of it all, but I know there is more to it than I can see. Even when Deda passed on. Thank You for allowing me to have the relationship I have with my grandfather. Thank You for putting him in my life and instilling wisdom and morals at such a young age.

I love Deda so much. It is such a blessing for little Tony to have Deda's name for a middle name. Right before Deda passed away, he said Tony was a boy, and we found out that Tony was a boy on the day Deda went. Lord, I thank You for arranging my life. I know I didn't know my dad that well, but the times I had with him were special. Deda was there when I was young, and I'm so thankful for that. I love them both, and I strongly believe that I will see them on the other side of this life.

Even the pregnancy was a battle. Megan had preeclampsia; she couldn't get an epidural for a while. Her contractions were crazy, and there were times when it just felt like the devil walked into the room and tried to throw everything he could at us. I remember praying to Jesus. During one of those prayers, I could see You writing in the sand like when the woman was being accused and she was about to be stoned. You wrote in the sand and told her accusers, "Let he who is without sin cast the first stone." When they dropped the stones and left, You said that You didn't accuse her either and to sin no more. I'm not completely sure I know what that means in my life, but there have been times where I have seen You writing in the sand.

I love You; thank You so much for comforting me. Thank You for the strength You gave Megan. She was so strong during her pregnancy. I don't know how she did it. I remember thinking, man how is she still pushing? I was tired, and I was just helping her push. Lord, she is so awesome. I love her more than words could express. Help me to express my love to her and not to be caught up in the pressures of this life and take it out on her. Help me to give her what she deserves: my love, respect, and reverence. She is so beautiful inside and out. Help me to show her that I see her beauty.

Tony was born around the time of three in the morning on April 29, 2009. He came into this world and all the pains of childbirth stopped. He was and is so beautiful. That was an awesome moment. I remember looking at Angela, Megan, and Tony. I was so overwhelmed with an unspeakable joy.

Thank You for allowing Angela to be there. She helped so much. I pray that You bless her life with the richness and fullness of Your grace. I also remember You asking if I was ready to see the depths of Your love. I would love to, my Lord.

After Tony's birth, I could feel a greater love for him and others. I realized that everyone is a child of someone else. I know that I love little Tony so much, and I would want him to be loved by everyone else. I couldn't imagine any mother or father wanting anything different for her or his child. On a deeper level, we are all Your children, Father, and we can only love from the portion You have given us according to what we can handle. We're not always ready to be loved, and in turn, love others. Your love is so much more in depth than the little portion we have. Even the little we have can be overwhelming at times, like experiencing the birth of my son, and yet You love us with Your love, which is limitless.

Lord,

Yesterday, the guys had questions about religion. One of these questions was about how come the Christians don't have the object of the cross and the Catholics do? This really stirred up something inside of me. This conversation led me to think about the importance of having a relationship with You. It is like this: if my son was interested in playing baseball and he joined a team called the Flyers would I see him as just a Flyer? No way; he is much more to me than a member of a baseball team. It is the same way with us. We are Your children. You created us and fashioned us in our mother's womb. You know our thoughts before we think them. You can count the hairs on our heads. You know how many times we lay down our heads to go to sleep. You even know how many times we have walked and will walk in this lifetime, because You know our comings and goings. We are the apples of Your eye. To You we are much more than a Christian, or a Baptist, or a Presbyterian. We are Your sons and daughters.

It seems like we try to put labels on things in order for us to understand what those things are. What if those things are beyond our understanding or beyond our labels? A person is so much deeper than that and so are You, Lord. For example, You are a healer, Jesus. You can heal the sick. Does that mean You are just a healer?

No way. You also raise the dead, walk on water, You can speak to the wind that stirs up the sea, and it will be silenced. You stand at the right hand of the Father. All things in the world were created for You, by You, and through You. Does that mean that You are just the Lord over heaven and Earth, master and ruler of all things? No, You are more than that. You even say that we are Your friends. You are not just a ruler of Your creation, but You are one with it. You are a friend to the meek, to those who mourn and are afflicted, to the widow and the orphan. Lord, You even know how they feel because You were afflicted, You were meek.

Two Become Three

You came down into the flesh became a person even though You are God Himself in order for us to be found in You. You can relate to the widow and the orphan, to be separated from the person who you invested your whole life into and poured out all of your love for and relied on. You were separated from Your Father when You took all the sin of mankind upon Yourself. You said, "My God, My God, why have you forsaken me (Matthew 27:41 NKJV)?" You are the shepherd and the lamb. Lord, You can't fit in a box. There is more to You than that and the people You have chosen to accept You as their Lord and Savior.

For those who are willing to let You be such a part of their lives. To be changed by the depths of Your love. For those who realize that Your love for them cannot only change them to have a love for You, but have a love for all people, including themselves and even their enemies. Those people—whether they are called a Catholic or a Protestant—don't fit into a box or label either. They are more than that, because they are one in You.

> Ezekiel 34:11–16 (NKJV)
> For thus saith the Lord God: "Indeed I myself will search for My sheep and seek them out. As a shepherd seeks out his flock on the day that he is among his scattered sheep, so will I seek out My sheep and deliver them from all the places where they were scattered on a cloudy and dark day. And I will bring them out from the peoples and gather them from the countries, and will bring them to their own land; I will feed them on the mountains of Israel, in the valleys and all the inhabited places of the country. I will feed them in good pasture, and their fold shall be on the high mountains of Israel. There they shall lie down in a good fold and feed in rich pasture on the mountains of Israel. I will feed my flock, and I

will make them lie down," says the Lord God. "I will seek what was lost and bring back what was driven away, bind up the broken and strengthen what was sick; but I will destroy the fat and the strong, and feed them in judgment."

You challenge my heart
My thoughts and my ways
So thankful for grace
That's leading me home
Into Your arms
You paid my price
It took Your life
You counted my loss
As a gain

Lord,

What is more profitable for me: to let go of my wealth in this earth and take hold of You, or to let go of my wealth when it is time to pass on and to have never taken hold of You?

Jesus,

You know how the prisoner feels. You know what it is like to be accused, to be put on trial, to be sentenced to death, to be executed for a crime. You were among the transgressors, except You didn't commit the crime You were accused of.

Jesus was found in humanity, so humanity would be found in Him.

Letter 2 of 3

Lord,

You are not a man that You should lie or the Son of Man that You should repent. You are the same yesterday, today, and forever. You are the beginning and the end. You are not like us. You do not cast a shifting shadow. You never change. You are who You are. You are steady, Lord. The things You say, You do. You carry it through. From generations to generations to generations. You have performed the things You have planned, even before You created the heavens, the earth, and everything in it. Your Word will truly last forever. I know this because You said it.

You have the nations in Your hand. Everything You have created is Yours, including us. Lord, Your feet can stand in a place where we would normally sink. Your ways are higher than our ways. Your love is beyond my comprehension. You know the very depths of my heart. I could fool the people around me for a brief moment, but I can never fool You. You know how I feel. You feel it with me. You feel my joy, my pain. Lord, You know. Thank You, Lord, for always being with me.

Thank You for loving me unconditionally, for believing in me. I love You, Jesus. You have always been faithful. You are steady in my life. Thank You, Lord. I praise You. You are above all I can imagine. You are my strength. You hold me up when I can't stand. You are my peace. The world can be crazy around me at times, but at the moment I think of You, the world stops. You come and dine with me. Your peace reminds me how good You are. I'm at peace when I am with You.

You are awesome! I fix my eyes on You. Lord, I want to see Your glory and feel Your presence in my life. The price You paid for me was not cheap. It cost Your life to attain me. Lord, when I try to hold myself up doing planks, it is tough after sixty seconds. Lord, only

Your hands and feet that were nailed to the cross held You up. The pain You felt on the cross I cannot imagine.

You were already torn open from the scourges. Your blood was spilt that I may live. Lord, You rescued me when I was in my worst condition. You took me into You. Lord, You are working Your righteousness in me. Thank You, Lord. Thank You. Thank You for Your mercy. I don't deserve Your mercy by the things that I do. You see me as the apple of Your eye. You are awesome, Lord. Thank You for loving me.

"[2A]Trust in me. [2B]I will never turn from you. [2C]Have faith in me, for I am God, the creator. [2D]My ways are higher than your thoughts. [2E]My people do not fear me. [2E]They mock me, they curse and slander my holy name. [2E]Their ways are far from mine. [2E]They see me as a joke, a byword, and their wicked ways have blinded them from the truth. I will crush their prejudices, disloyalty, promiscuity, backbiting, envy, bitterness, greed, and pride beneath my feet, for I, the Lord, have spoken. (Spoken to where I was from the Holy Spirit)

"My son, this shaking that you have in your prayers is what I plan to do to the earth beneath your feet. The word that Megan received was from me. I will come to her and your son in visions. They will prophesy in my name, for I am the Lord God who visits the iniquity of those who despise my name. They pervert my truth and go whoring with statues and false ideas. They have created their own version of who I am so they can feel good about the wickedness they orchestrate in this land. (Spoken to where I was from the Holy Spirit)

"[2F]Have they forgot that I created the land they live in? [2G]Have they forgot that the blood of the innocent stains the land to a point where the land vomits them out of its mouth? [2G]I am sick of the perverseness of this generation. [2H]They act as if I don't see, as if I don't hear. [2H]Have they forgot that I have created eyes and ears, that the same senses were made in my likeness?

"When I shake the earth, many will die (Spoken to where I was from the Holy Spirit). For I am the Lord God and I have spoken. I will move with haste to see that the words I have spoken will come to pass (Spoken to where I was from the Holy Spirit). [2J]Repent from your sins, turn from your wickedness, and turn to me. [2K]Learn from me, for the fear of the Lord is the beginning of wisdom. [2L]I will save those who call upon my name. [2M]For I am the Lord God. [2N]I am slow to anger and full of compassion for those who put their trust in me. [2O]I have saved you from sin. [2P]I took your sin upon myself when I died on Golgotha Hill. [2P]I bore my cross.

"[2Q]You must bare yours to follow me, for sorrow may last a night, but joy will come in the morning. [2R]Your existence in this fallen world is as fragile as a whisper in the ears of men, but the inheritance I give to those who put their trust in me is eternal. [2S]Trust in me, for I am the Lord God, ruler of the heavens and the earth."

This is a letter that was written for my sister's friends. They had recently lost a friend, and God urged me to write this letter. He would tell me that if I wrote it, He would speak through it. It took me around three days to finally write it, but this is what came out.

Letter 3 of 3

I know you might not know me. My name is Anthony Diamandi. I'm Ashley's brother. Around nine years ago, I started an adventure with Jesus Christ, and He changed my life forever. He rescued me from drugs, alcohol, sexual addictions, suicide, hatred, confusion, isolation, and destruction. For about seventy percent of my life, I turned my back on the Lord and followed the devil. All the while not knowing that the devil's plans for my life were to steal, kill, and destroy.

On the outside I probably looked normal, but on the inside, I felt empty and lonely, even when I was in a room full of friends. I felt dead inside. The things that used to be fun for me became weights that were impossible to carry and hard to get rid of. I always felt that I would walk into a situation that I couldn't get out of and the situation would have led to drastic consequences that would affect my life and the ones I love forever.

It was at the perfect time that Jesus used everything around me, my friends, my friends' parents, the Bible, even the ocean, and the Holy Spirit speaking directly to my heart to draw me back to him. It took many prayers over my life. I wrote God a letter, asking Him to show me that He was working in my life and three days later, I got washed through the Main Street Pier. I hit four poles without getting one scratch on my body. I was in a band called LBO.

The first verse in one of our songs was, "so here I am reaching out of the water so I don't drown." That was how I felt in my life—like I was always trying to keep my head above water. That night, I sang that song for about the hundredth time. This time it had new meaning, because God put me in the song literally at the Main Street Pier.

I dedicated my life to finding out who this God was and following Him. It has been an amazing journey in a short time and Ashley can verify the change that has taken place in my life. I've lived in Japan. I have a loving family, a wonderful wife and an awesome little son. These are treasures I would have never known if I had taken a drug that my body just couldn't handle, or if I would have gotten into a fight with someone who didn't care whether I lived or died, or if I would have fallen asleep behind the wheel. Our lives are so fragile and my biggest blessing was that Jesus Christ was always with me, protecting me and revealing His deep love for me. I see Him doing the same things with you. You see, He doesn't treat us differently. He loves us all the same.

I used to think that all the bad things that took place in my life, He could have prevented. I realize right now as I'm writing to you that if God would have prevented those things from happening, I couldn't relate to you. I would have nothing to write to you now because I would have never been in similar situations. I write to you in Jesus's name. God loves you with a love that cannot be measured.

"[3A]I have been walking with you from the very moment I created you. [3B]Everything I create is beautiful to me and you are my creation. [3C]You are my sons and daughters. [3D]Come to me all who carry heavy burdens and cannot rest. [3E]Take my weight upon you for it is light. [3E]I come to give you rest. [3F]I'm asking you to trust me. [3G]There is meaning to life. I know you have been asking that question. [3H]I hear your thoughts my sons and my daughters. [3I]I have counted your tears. [3J]I cry when you cry. [3K]I laugh when you laugh. [3L]You are my children.

"[3M]You are here to have a relationship with me and to love each other as I love you. [3N]Come to me and I will strengthen you. [3O]Learn my ways and teach others about my Son. [3P]You see, my kingdom has no end.

"[3Q]In my Son all things were created and I give Him to you. [3R]He sacrificed His life that you may live in me forever. [3S]He took the sins of the world upon Himself. [3S]He did this for all humanity from the beginning to the end to have a chance to be saved from sin. [3S]The pain He took upon himself for your sake, I could not bear to watch. [3T]My love for you is found in Him and it never runs empty.

"[3U]You have been trusting in wells that have holes in them. [3U]They run dry. [3V]Follow me, for I am the way, the truth, and the life. [3W]I come to give you peace and life in abundance. [3X]Yes, you will have troubles in this world, but have no fear, for I have overcome the world. [3Y]I am the Prince of Peace.

"[3Z]What does it profit a man to gain the whole world but to lose his soul, you see if you put your trust in things that are not found in me, they will only let you down; you are meant and created to

Letters in Vessels

experience deeper things. ³ᴬ³I have great plans for each and every one of you. ³ᴮ³Use them for my glory and I will honor you. ³ᶜ³I have created you for a purpose.

"³ᴰ³Seek me and I will speak to you as I speak to you now. ³ᴱ³Seek and you will find, ask and you will receive, come to me. ³ᶠ³I love you. ³ᴳ³I am with you. ³ᴴ³My heart burns for you.

"³ᴵ³I will be your strength and your song. ³ᶠ³You have to come to me as you are. ³ᴶ³I will heal you and rescue you from the great waters, pains and afflictions just as I did with Israel. ³ᴺYou have to come to me. ³ᴷ³Talk to me through prayer. ³ᴸ³Love each other and learn my words. ³ᵐ³My words are life. ³ᴺ³They will be lamps to your feet and lights to your path. ³ᴼ³I come to give you direction, hope and assurance that I hear you, that I know you. ³ᴾ³That I call you by the name I named you. ³Q³I have never and will never forsake you. ³ᴿ³I know that man has let you down. ³ˢ³I am not a man that I should lie. ³ᵀ³I will never give up on you.

"³ᵁ³I am the greatest treasure you could ever have and you are my greatest treasure. ³ⱽ³Just as I have laid down my everything for you, my very own Son, I want you to lay down everything for me and you will realize that I am everything that you are looking for. ³ᵂ³Love and follow me with all of your heart, mind, soul and love each other. ³ˣ³Everything falls under those two things."

14

Nimitz Letters

Near the end of the year 2009, my tour in Atsugi, Japan was about to end. During that time, the Navy had a policy called "high year tenure." If a member of the Navy could not make the rank of E-5 (Second-Class Petty Officer) within eight years, they would have to get out of the Navy honorably. I saw several good sailors who wanted to keep their jobs get out that way. I was next. I had one test left. If I could not make rank on that test, I would have to leave the same way.

I took the test and prepared mentally for getting out and staying in. I still was not sure what the Lord wanted me to do. I made rank on that test by the skin of my teeth. When they drew the line for those who made rank, I landed with one foot on the line and the other foot on the side that made rank. I did not make rank by a full point. My score was around point eight past the set score.

I was now an E-5 Second Class Petty Officer in the Navy with the options of either staying or getting out. Megan and I had a little boy and the decision seemed to carry more weight this time. I did not want to stay, but I did want to follow the Lord's will. I prayed on it. I felt like He wanted me to stay in. I still kept asking Him what to do. I was walking to work one day and I could feel the Lord speaking to my heart. The same way He spoke to me before the first letter. It was not loud, instead still and soft. In its quietness everything within me was connected to it and heard it. He told me to look into their eyes and tell Him they were not worth it. I knew what He wanted me to do.

He wanted me to look into the eyes of the guys I was working with and see if their lives were worth me sticking around. I did look into their eyes that day and knew what I had to do. I was not sure how me sticking around was going to help these guys or the guys I would encounter in the Navy in the future. Most of the time. I felt like I was on the fringe, hanging on to Jesus's garment or by His tomb, crying to have his dead body back after He had already risen.

I still feel that way to this day, but "with God all things are possible (Matthew 19:26 NKJV)." Just like Moses asking God how He would be a spokesperson for Israel while having a speech impediment. God told Moses that He made the mouth, so it would be easy for Him to speak through the mouth of Moses.

> 1 Corinthians 1:27 (NKJV)
> "But God has chosen the foolish things of the world to put to shame the wise; and God has chosen the weak things of the world to put to shame the things which are mighty."

I reenlisted for five more years: from 2010-2016. I began my third tour on the USS Nimitz (CVN 68), another aircraft carrier that was stationed in San Diego for six months. After that six months, the Nimitz would move to its homeport in Everett, Washington. During that time, we would move back and forth from Everett to Bremerton between deployments and dry dock for upkeep on the ship. The letters below were written during those times.

Truth will not yield to our convenience. It is what it is.

Romans 8:18 (NKJV)
"For I consider that the suffering of this present time are not worthy to be compared with the glory which will be revealed in us."

Matthew 4:6 (NKJV)
"Blessed are those which do hunger and thirst for righteousness, for they shall be filled."

Romans 8:10–11 (NKJV)
And if Christ be in you, the body is dead because of sin, but the Spirit is life because of righteousness. But if the Spirit of Him who raised Jesus from the dead dwell in you. He who raised Christ from the dead will also give life to your mortal bodies through His Spirit that dwells in you.

John 8:36 (NKJV)
"Therefore if the son makes you free, you shall be free indeed."

Romans 8:14–17 (NKJV)
For as many as are led by the Spirit of God, these are sons of God. For you did not receive the Spirit of bondage again to fear, but you received the Spirit of adoption by whom we cry out, "Abba, Father." The Spirit Himself bears witness with our spirit that we are children of God, and if children, then heirs-heirs of God and joint heirs with Christ, if indeed we suffer with Him, that we may also be glorified together.

Lord,

When I opened this notebook, I read the notes I took from the Rock, confess everything to Jesus. Lord, it has been a long time since I have written to You. Help me write to You in truth and in spirit. You are showing me so much today. Thank You. This morning I was talking to the man at the kiosk. He said he went to church. I could see Your love in his eyes.

We were talking about how everything works in cohesion with each other. We used examples of the ship and how much entails just with the guy who orders the food and how cruise ships use power and if every plug was plugged in, would the weakest piece of equipment short circuit, and how he won tickets to the Padres and the road he passed by every day that he never used he now had to use to get the Padres tickets. He never knew that the road existed until he had to use it and it was right around the corner from his house. Lord, help me learn Your teachings in these conversations. I could see that You were in our conversation. Bless that man, be with him in a strong way.

There was another man who was on the trolley with me. He was such a cool man. He is a contracted bouncer and doesn't like his job very much. He said that he wished he had a plan that he stuck with and that his plans changed according to who he wanted to be at the time. Lord, I pray You give him direction and show him Your plans in his life. The past week has been tough and awesome, mixed with sufferings and moments where that breaks and your presence is strong. I feel Your presence so strong and it feels so good to be close to You. Lord Jesus, I love You. Thank You for taking hold of my hands. Thank You for pressing Your head against mine and praying to our father on my behalf. Thank You that I'm Yours and nothing can take me from You.

Those who You set free are free indeed. Thank You that my sister is Ashley; she is so cool and such a little light and a straight shooter. Lord, comfort her, visit her as much as You can; show her that You have a deep love for her. Encourage her, Lord. Bless her life. Jesus, help her understand the depths of Your sacrifice for her. Get personal with her and show her Your intimacy and how You create those circumstances for her to get to know You in a personal way. And how You have those plans for her and her alone.

Lord, bless Megan and Tony. Help Megan come to You for advice on how to raise Tony. Help them to understand each other, Lord. Lead Megan with Your spirit. Help Tony's spiritual ears, eyes, hands, and feet to be able to hear, see, feel, and run to You even at a young age and throughout his whole life. I pray that we will be able to unite spiritually even when we are apart physically. I lost my Bible today. I pray that whoever picks it up will be blessed and changed by You. Use it for Your glory.

I know You have been stripping things away from me that don't belong to You and this chastisement when it comes it comes from a Father who cares deeply for his son. Lord, help me to let all those things go, to learn quick and to know that those times are bringing me closer to You. Help me to cling to You and thank You for breaking me gently. I pray for Your peace to enter the city of San Diego. Encourage Lee. Love on him; cover him with Your grace and mercy. You fight for him and nothing can stand against You. You are Lord of heavenly hosts (armies).

Lord, love Mom. Strengthen her and fill her with Your love. Show her that You are with her every step and that You always have been with her. Lord, I love You; be with Angela, Tara, Cody, and David. Breathe on them, Lord. Lead them by Your spirit. Bless them.

December 2012

The only words I could say about the shootings in Connecticut are not even my own.

"⁷Man's inhumanity to man makes countless thousands mourn." (Bentman and Burns, "Man Was Made to Mourn," The Poetical Works of Burns.36.)

Lord,

Thank You for the measures You take to reach us Your children. For the trials You bring Your saints through that the Word may be planted in the hearts of men. Paul was stoned, scourged, and shipwrecked with one intention: that Your love and message the gospel, that Jesus would be revealed in the hearts of men.

2 Corinthians 11:23–28

Lord,

I believe, help me believe. You're gracious and faithful. Your mercy endures forever. Lord, I trust You. I know that You got this and You're in control. Thank You for saving my life from eternal consumption. I love You and praise You. You are so faithful. I praise You, Lord Jesus. Thank You for the cross, for dying, and for taking the nails, the insults, the punches to the face and the mocking.

Your clothes were gambled away. Your flesh was torn off and ripped from Your body. Lord, thank You so much. You know what it is like to suffer. Wherever I go, You have gone before me and have experienced these things. Help me to embrace the cross. To know the privilege, I share in Your sufferings, that I may share in Your overcoming, Your resurrection.

Lord, You died and rose. You stepped out of the grave. I love You so much. Help me be more intimate with You, to experience Your love. Your grace is sufficient. No weapon against us shall prosper. If You are for us, who could ever be against us, and nothing can separate us from Your love, not even death, spiritual principalities, or powers.

I pray that You clear the air and replace it with the fruits of Your spirit. Lord, I pray that I can drink from Your fountains of everlasting waters. To feed on Your spirit. To commune and sup with You. To look into Your eyes and experience the warmth of Your love. It feels so good to talk with You and open up to You. I'm sorry it's not always like this. Help me come to You more often.

Lord,
    You are holy and just. Your Word is a lamp to my feet and a light to my path. Lord, I seek You in a dark place and whatever fights against me is ultimately fighting against You and You have overcome the world. I know that You are Lord of hosts.
    Thousands upon thousands of angels, and You fight for us. Lord, open my eyes to see the chariots that fight for me. God, I love You and I thank You for Your love, for Your grace. Lord, You are good and just. I praise You and magnify You. You are glorious.
    Come fill this place with Your glory. You are triumphant and holy. Come in our midst. Help us to see You, Lord. Clear the air. Remove the obscenities and blasphemies. Send praise in its place. You inhabit the praise of Your people.
    You are my comforter and my strong tower. I look to You, the author and finisher of my faith. Help me to take shelter in You, to be huddled under Your wings where there is healing. Your grace is sufficient. In my weakness Your strength is revealed. No weapon formed against me shall prosper. If You are for me, who could ever be against me? The heart is evil above all things. Lord, cure the sin-sick heart, bring the dross to the surface, and scoop out whatever offends You.

Lord,
    This is not my home. I don't belong here. You came into the world You created, and it didn't even recognize You or even acknowledge You because its works were evil. It was so consumed in darkness that it was too blind to see that You are the light of men. That in

You is life. That in You, Jesus is the only way to have a relationship with Father God.

Help me to see You in truth and in spirit, to walk in Your love. My inner ears, in my soul I will listen, take in and digest what You have to say. Help me to be like Moses and Joshua. Help me to talk to You as a man talks to his friend. Help me to go to You for instruction. Help me to lay down at Your feet and just bask in Your glorious presence in the radiance of Your righteousness.

Help me to soak in Your love. Help me lay my head on Your chest and listen to Your heartbeat. You are faithful and just and true and beautiful. You are God.

> "When the power of love overcomes the love of power, the world will know peace." ([8]Hendrix, Brainy quotes. http://www-brainyquotes/Jimi_Hendrix_195397)

Is it worth it for me to choose power, to get to the highest position, to work all my life and not to experience the important things like relationships? I can sacrifice those things and hurt the people I want to get ahead of. For what? A position, fame, money, acceptance? All of those things I will have to leave behind when I die. Like Job said, he had nothing when he came into this world and he will have nothing when he goes.

Even if I attained the power I was seeking, would that really fulfill me or would I always be hungry for the next level of? I will never be full. A wise man once said that all good things come from God. I think it was John the Baptist. Lord, I don't want power or anything that is not given to me from Your hand for Your glory. Anything else would be like building my future on soft sand.

When water and wind come, my future would crash to the ground because the foundation was so weak. Lord, help me to build all things on Your very words. What I build never will fall. It will be solid.

Lord, I don't want to live in vain. Just chasing the wind. I want my life to have meaning, to have purpose. I want You to look at me on the day I go to see You and say, "Well done, good and faithful servant." Lord, thank You for Your deep love. Thank You so much for opening my eyes to see You. Even though it's just in glimpses, it is enough to change my life forever. Word of life, let Your grace lead us home to the place that You prepare for us.

Lord,
   Let me rest my head on Your heart. On the inside, in the guts there is a fight for blood. Dark and light tear each other apart and try to pull each other out of my mouth. On the outside, all prepare for the consuming fire to come. Some work to hold onto everything they got. Some get ready to let it all go.
   Your love is strong. Inside of You is peace. Lord, You are a fortress and a strong tower. It is crazy in this world where we make our own plans against You. It creates a cancer in the air that tries to permeate us and get into our insides. Lord, rebellion is witchcraft in Your sight. At first it looks appealing, but it is sin and sin leads to death. Jesus, You are the resurrection and the life.
   I know that inside of You is like Moses crawling into the cleft of the rock safe from the wrath that is to come. You are a sanctuary. Lord, I know I don't understand it, it hurts. I do question it. You of all know. It is a cross. Your grace is sufficient. I know You are at work in this. You are doing mighty things in the unseen. You move in darkness, and You provide the moon at night and sun in the day.
   You provide light in the dark. You don't leave us in darkness. Your Word is a lamp to my feet and a light to my path. I know that our faces will shine brighter than the sun and joy will come in the morning. You give us a garment of praise for the spirit of heaviness.

Letters in Vessels

Vision:

In it I can hear a large amount of people's thoughts, not sure how many maybe hundreds. Their thoughts are all over the place. About what they should do, should have done, or should be doing. What they think about others. All of these thoughts are running circles in their minds and these thoughts aren't directed to anyone but those thinking them.

Although they should have been directed to the one, the only one who could help. These thoughts are bringing such a heaviness in my heart. When I wonder will they have any peace from these thoughts or will they find it, I see a giant cross. The heaviness of all these thoughts are lifted. I see a couple of people walk up to the cross, look at it baffled and they walked off with their thoughts. It was like they didn't want to let go of it.

> "Stand for something or fall for anything." (⁹Doyle, Mieder, Shapiro, The Dictionary of Modern Proverbs, 239.)

Lord,

Help me stand in You. I know that You are the rock in the parable that the man built his house upon. The storms came and beat on the house. That house stood because of its foundation. I pray for a life that stands in You and with You always. I love You, Jesus. I know You stood with Shadrach, Meshach, and Abednego in the heat and flames of raging fire. Stand with me like that.

I love You, Lord, and praise You. I know Your hand is strong and no one can be plucked out of it. You supply all my needs. That is so cool that on the other side of this life, I will praise You in the fullness of your glory. I will be with them and all who follow You into sleep in You until they rise.

I need You with me and in me by Your spirit more than anything. I know You are because You say it and Your word is solid.

What You speak You will follow through on it. Lord, Your grace is sufficient. You loved us first. You are love. Lord, my innermost desire away from You is to serve myself. I would hurt myself and anyone around me to have my need met. Away from You, that is exactly where that living—or should I say dying—will lead me, away from You. I don't want that.

Lord,
You're faithful. You understand, and You know all things. You satisfy my soul. Comfort Tony, help him understand even at a young age that you are with him and that You are in this. Lord, I pray that Your love will break through like many waters and saturate little man's soul. I pray that you show him and Megan that I love them very much while I'm out in this ocean. I trust You, Father. I know that You never leave us nor forsake us. Bless them Lord. Bring them the joy of knowing You.

Punk 102
Megan's buddy said that Megan was a punker for Jesus. She said she could imagine Megan throwing safety pins at the devil. I like that. Back in the day, I wrote a report in high school called Punk 101. The report was about punks seeing what was wrong in society. They saw the hypocrisy in the world and in their homes and rebelled.

They broke the mold of the image they were held to be by their families and society. In that report I wrote something about the kid who sees the cookie jar and is told not to touch it. The punks were the ones who grab the cookie jar because they know the cookie tastes good. I also wrote about the Sex Pistols and how, when a man in America heard them on television, he broke his television set. I wrote about how they were attacked by a group of people with machetes because of the music they played.

If I was to continue that paper, I would call it Punk 102. I would write it from a different perspective, different eyes. It would go something like this. The punks did see the truth about the hypocrisy around them. Sid Vicious and Johnny Rotten's real names were Simon Richie and John Lydon. They could see that the things they did like singing, "God Save the Queen" and "I am the Antichrist" pissed people off.

These antics would reveal an ugliness in people who probably acted like that wasn't in them. The problem with this for the punks was while they were pointing this out to show that it wasn't right, the same types of behavior were multiplying and manifesting in their own lives. This is something I'm almost positive they didn't want. It was just all they knew. They were becoming, feeding in and off what they hated.

Another thing about the punks was they would say to be yourself and do whatever you want to do. This is what I thought was so cool about punk rock. There were no rules; you could make them and be who you wanted to be. The problem with this idea is that if you believe in no rules and you believe that you can make your own, even if you are making your own, there are still rules.

This is how so many different groups came about. There was and still are groups such as: straight edge, hardcore, emo, old school, just to name a few. So how could a young punk say there are no rules and then make them, hypocrisy? The very thing they hated in the first place. Do whatever you want and be yourself also doesn't sit right with me because do we human beings really know what we want and who we are? Aren't we figuring these things out as we go?

Okay, I'm not trying to bash the punks. I am one myself. I would not know anything about this movement if I didn't live it. I'm still in it, just in a different way. I will explain this later. This is where I came out of. They are a part of me and I am a part of them. I can't just point them out like that and leave them in judgment, but I do see holes in the philosophy and I'm using these holes to point to Jesus. He was punk.

He saw the hypocrisy as well and realized it was in us all. He gave Himself to clear it out of us, out of our lives and replace it with a peace that only He has. He gives us the joy that was set before Him. Jesus, the real Jesus, not the Jesus Simon Richie and John Lydon saw in their parents and society. That is not the real Jesus. That is a wolf dressed up in sheep's clothing. That is a front.

If they would have seen Jesus as He really is, they would have seen that He was the missing piece to their whole scene. Those things that they despised, He despised too. He came to take it out of their scene and out of them as well. Was Jesus radical? He was radical just on what He claimed and what He did.

Jesus claimed to be the Son of God. He claimed that He was the only way to the Father: "I am the way, the truth, and the life(John 14:6 NKJV)." He claimed that He could forgive sins, that He would be betrayed, crucified, and would rise from the dead. He claimed to have come from heaven. He claimed to be the Messiah, the one all the prophets spoke of. The one that Moses showed as a sign when the snake was lifted up, that he would be lifted up. The one that Abraham's life was a sign when God told him to kill his only son. God provided the sacrifice. Jesus claimed that He was the lamb, the ultimate sacrifice. He claimed that He was the fulfillment of the law.

He went to the synagogue and even said the scripture was being fulfilled before their eyes. He walked into the synagogue and flipped the merchant's tables over. He stood up for the lady that was caught in adultery, "Who that is without sin, cast the first stone.(John 8:7 NKJV)" He went to eat with Zacchaeus, the man that had to climb a tree because no one would let him get close to Jesus. Jesus came to him. Jesus would speak to demons and they would flee.

Jesus told us to pick up our cross. He said that if we cling to our lives, we would lose them, but He also said for us to give our lives and we would gain them back. He was the one who said the widow with the two coins gave the most because it was all she had. He would heal people with a touch.

Letters in Vessels

Some of those people had been afflicted with ailments more than half their lives. He saw things in people that no one else could see. He hung out with prostitutes and tax collectors who were seen as thieves in Israel. He saw that the centurion had great faith because the man said that Jesus could send a word to heal his servant.

Jesus walked on water, opened the eyes of the blind, healed on the Sabbath, spoke to an unsettled sea and the sea was calmed. He healed His enemies like the guard that came to arrest him. He fed thousands with a couple of fish and some bread. He claimed that if people didn't believe Him for what He said, they should believe Him for the things He did. He told the Roman governor that He didn't have power unless it was given by Jesus's father.

Was He radical? He rose Lazarus from the grave. He glowed in front of His disciples so much His clothes were whiter than any clothes that could be laundered. He claimed that whoever came to Him and believed in Him would be set free from sin and death. He claimed that He was before Moses. He said that He didn't have a place to lay His head. He said that He was the bread of life and that man would go hungry on regular food. He said if we came to Him, we would never go hungry.

He claimed that He had living waters and that whoever would come to Him for water would never thirst again. He was the one who said if your eye causes you to sin, pluck it out. He said if your hand causes you to sin, cut it off. He said to forsake your family for Him. He said that it was easier for a camel to get through the eye of a needle than for a rich person to get into heaven.

He told His disciples that whoever desired to be the greatest must become the least. He claimed that He would come down from the clouds. His kingdom would have no end. He claimed that His kingdom had no end, that we would be judged by the words He spoke. He also washed the disciple's feet and rode in on a donkey.

Was Jesus radical? He walked before men and they would give up everything to follow Him. All of His disciples except for John were crucified, beheaded, thrown off the temple because they knew what they saw and wouldn't recant on what Jesus had done in their lives. Jesus took the stripes, forty lashes, and still stood up to carry the cross He would hang on. After He died, He stepped out of His tomb and walked around with His people with the holes in His hands and feet. Talk about radical! Talk about punk rock!

> Matthew 12:31-32 (NKJV)
> Therefore I say to you, every sin and blasphemy will be forgiven men, but the blasphemy against the Holy Spirit will not be forgiven men. Anyone who speaks a word against the Son of Man, it will be forgiven him; but whoever speaks against the Holy Spirit, it will not be forgiven him, either in this age or the age to come.

Jesus was sticking up for the Holy Spirit. The religious leaders were saying that Jesus cast out devils by the devil. Jesus said that a kingdom divided against itself wouldn't stand. In other words, if the devil is against himself by casting himself out, his kingdom would not stand. Then Jesus said that if He Himself cast out devils by the Spirit of God, then the Kingdom of Heaven has come upon them.

The Spirit of God is the Holy Ghost. Jesus was revealing His divinity through the power of the Holy Ghost. The Holy Ghost is one of the three persons in the Trinity. We would never know the power of Jesus if it wasn't revealed through His works.

For example; if Jesus didn't heal the sick, raise the dead, cast out devils, rise from the dead—you get my point, if I keep going it will be forever—He would just be another man with a lot to say and nothing to back it up. A bagpipe—plenty of air but that is about it.

John 21:25 (NKJV)
And there are also many other things that Jesus did, which if they were written one by one, I suppose that even the world itself could not contain the books that would be written. Amen.

Jim's father was right. If we don't give the Holy Ghost the credit He deserves, we put a stop to Him revealing the Son, Jesus. In turn, we put a stop to Jesus revealing the Father, God. Jesus said every sin will be forgiven, even blaspheming the Son of Man.

It is like this: a child must crawl before he walks and must walk before he runs. A child could say he wants to walk or run, but if that child says he doesn't want to crawl, he will never crawl, walk, or run. They all lead into each other. The Father (run), the Son (walk), and the Holy Ghost (crawl). The Holy Ghost is that breath that God blows into man, giving man life and allows Him to see God. Without that breath, man would be dead to God, not knowing Him.

If we were to blaspheme the Son Jesus, the Holy Ghost would be there to reveal Him. If we blaspheme the Holy Ghost, we snuff out our only revelator of Jesus. You can say you don't want to walk or run, but not to worry, the crawl will get you ready for the walk and the walk for the run. My point is the crawl is still there. Without it, you wouldn't know the other two. The Holy Ghost always spoke of Jesus and Jesus always spoke of His Father.

For Tony

My son,
There are so many things I want to tell you to prepare you in life, but we will have to take it one step at a time. I pray that Jesus will walk on the waters when they rage inside and outside of you. I pray He will say the words to calm the sea and that He will help you to see that these seasons are temporary.

Lord,

I need You and Your truth to cut through and bring revelation to things I don't understand. God, I know You know all things and that You are in this. Help me to be real with You and come to You open, in truth, and by Your spirit. God, there are two things that seem to be going on. For one, it feels like the devil is accusing me, coming fierce with my flaws, and trying to stun me like a deer in the headlights to try to stop me from doing what needs to be done. Half the time, I don't even know what needs to be done.

I feel like there are thousands of lies all around me and in me. My flesh wants to believe in the lies and run with them, but there is one truth that can set me free from all those lies. In the midst of all this, that one truth is hard to see, like a needle in the haystack. Lord, it seems like the wickedness of the wicked is prevailing and setting an atmosphere that is blinding, breathtaking, and life-threatening eternally. Lord, cut through the atmosphere like a fault line and let the tremors break up the evil.

The other thing is that in all of this, You feel far away even when You are not. It also feels, and just being real Lord, like You are chastening me and using these events to allow me to see that I have many issues that need Your touch, like a testing. To see if my heart chooses You through it all, like You are breaking me gently. You are close to the broken and contrite in spirit. Like You are using this to keep me humble, that I might run to You in my brokenness.

Lord, You're the only one who knows all these things going on within me before I even think them or write them down, and I'm sorry for choosing man. The ones around me and myself to run to when I should be running to You. It feels like we are about to hit a port and a large part of the ship are speaking out plans into the air that war against You. Spiritual wickedness, principalities, and rulers of this region are taking these plans as a gateway to spew evil on us and instigate even more plans to be spoken out which allows them to do their work. God, bind these plans and the devil's ability to move in these plans. Lord, bind the strong man. Let Your will be done on Earth as it is heaven.

>
> Open me up
> Fill the cup
> Stir the waters
> Set up a front
> For the one who goes to steal
> Your sons and daughters
> And the devil
> He doesn't have a problem with me
> He's got a grudge with you
> He tries to use who you love
> To do what he do

Lord,

Your ways are higher than our ways. We are dust. We come from it and return back to it. Our understanding of You is watered down, delusional. The only way we can have understanding of who You really are is through You, by Your spirit. Our hearts are wicked desperately. We try to build temples to ourselves.

We follow each other blindly and wonder why we are left empty and needing more. Even when we hurt the ones we love and the just to make our dreams come true. The ways of man are sin, and sin leads to death. We try to build our kingdoms in sand, in dust, because it is all we know. It is who we are. The winds and the water move the dust and our kingdom falls.

I praise You God that Your kingdom is coming. It is not built with human hands. It is not established on sand. You built it on Your own Son, Jesus, the rock. His kingdom won't fall when shaken. It will stand forever. It is what we are all looking for, but we can't get it on our terms. We are not God, You are. We didn't make You, You made us. On Your terms.

Lord,

You do not condemn. You do not hold our sins against us. You hold our sins against Yourself. Our sins are obliterated by Your righteousness and glory.

Your grace is sufficient. You are love. You are faithful and true. My peace is in You, the prince of it. I love You, Lord. You are my peace in the valley. Thank You that You are with me.

February 2015

Vision:

I'm in the dark, on my knees, head in my hands. Although my eyes are closed and covered by my hands, I can see Jesus Christ standing in the dark and it is raining all around us. My inner eyes are fixed on Him and He is staring into my soul. Eyes of fire, but gentle and understanding at the same time. All of a sudden, we are standing in an air pocket in the depths of a dark blue sea and the water around us is still and calming. He takes His hands in the shape of a bowl and scoops up water in front of His feet.

He takes this water and begins to pour it into my hands. I look into my hands and can see the water filling in my hands, forming ripples like sets of waves. I can also see the reflection in the water is not mine. It is the reflection of Jesus. He is no longer standing next to me. He is in the water. I stick my tongue in the water, and I can see one drop of water rolling off the back of my tongue and falling into a dark pit.

When the drop hits the bottom, I can feel a puddle of life resting at the bottom of my bowels the very bottom of my belly where my soul is sucking it up. I start to drink the rest of this water and can feel Jesus sprouting and rising inside of me like the shoot of a plant. All around Him is the rest of me fighting it, kicking and screaming style. I finish drinking until Jesus fills me to the brim. I can see through His eyes now that I'm standing in the rain and I see a person in the dark with His head in His hands looking at me from the inside.

Lord in Your strength
My weakness is strong
Why do I cling to this darkness so long?
And run to the hurt
To run away from the hurt
When You're the one who's breath
Brings life to the dirt

Religion: Man's way of man getting close to God.
Relationship: God's way of man getting close to God.
These were my last letters while in the Navy on active duty.

April 2016

At the end of my tour on the USS Nimitz, I missed rank on my last exam as a Second Class Petty Officer. I had to get out of active service honorably in the Navy on higher tenure. I did not make the rank of E-6 by fourteen years. Not long after that, around 2017, I signed up to be a Construction Electrician for the SEABEES in the reserves. I have also been working as a Securitas security officer at Sound Transit Light Rail train stations in Seattle, Washington.

15

I Live For You in Dedication to Her

January 20, 2019

Lord,
This one is going to be hard to write.

I sat down at church trying to make sense of it all. The sermon in the back of my torn mind did not seem to give me any of the answers I was looking for. The night before I lost the inspiration for this book. I lost the inspiration for me coming to know You, Lord. The one who showed me that I was truly genuinely loved and showed me that I could love back. Megan, my sweet angel, the love of my life, my soulmate, and best friend went to sleep and never woke up.

I did. I don't know how or the reason why I have made it to write these words down. Maybe part of the reason is to write these words down. These words, this writing is a gift. The hardest, most excruciating, gut-wrenching times of my life have brought the words out. The writing comes through after these times.

It is like something breaks the turmoil and words come out as sweet as honey from the carcass of a lion who just tried to devour me. I still don't know how or why I'm still alive. Maybe to write these words, take care of my boy, give my all and get home to the kingdom You are preparing for me. On my way there, I can leave some breadcrumbs for family, friends, loved ones, and even my enemies. A trail that leads to You, Lord, for future generations. I think that ultimately, I'm making my way back home where I can dance with my beautiful wife in the fullness of Your glory. Where it will all finally fully make sense.

I sat in church too numb to cry and trying to make sense of it all. The sermon ended and worship began. There were concerns I had which I could not express to You in words or thoughts. My heart was so crushed that my mind stopped thinking to comfort my heart. It was like my mind stopped thinking and walked down from my head to my chest to give my heart a hug. Your spirit intercedes on my behalf. Your spirit reveals my groans, the things I can't sort out and presents them to You clear as crystal.

In my depths, I was crying out to You, hoping Megan made it into Your arms, into Your kingdom on the other side of this life. My soul was longing to see that she made it home. I had my head in my hands, and the tears started flowing. I was with You once again with water all around us. This had happened once in my life before. It felt like I was being held with You and by You in a raindrop.

I thought to You my wish of Megan being okay and all of a sudden, I could see a magenta color shooting and zipping all around us. I could see it through the walls of water on the other side. Outside of the raindrop. I asked You without words what the magenta was, but I already knew the answer to that question.

It was Megan. She was twirling and gliding all around us. I asked You without words if I could have a moment with her. At that moment, she floated over to the raindrop and pressed against it from her side. I could see her beautiful mixture of purple, violet, red, and pink through the wash of water that was between us. I pressed my head against the water on my side of the raindrop. We leaned into each other through the water. In an instant, I could feel Megan. Her beauty, grace, gentle touch, her joy, her sweet smell, her tenderness, her love was gently easing my mind. I didn't want to leave that moment. This seemed to last about thirty seconds before she zipped off, flying in circles like a streamer in the wind.

It was a beautiful sight to see her so free, happy, and not bound by her earthly body. In the last years of her life she was in a brutal battle with anorexia. Lord, You know this. We called anorexia ED. It was terrible to have ED around, but who Megan was and the way she handled the hardest times of her life was the most beautiful thing I have or will ever see. She had Aspergilloma, a couple of lung surgeries in the past from the Aspergilloma and the root canal the night she passed. Her body was too weak from ED and the surgeries. In those last years, her aura and persona just got brighter, more loving which I thought was impossible for her to get more loving than she already was. She proved me wrong. The way she quietly battled the mental and physical strain of ED was the most inspiring thing. She would walk into a room, and if you were the one on her radar, you were the most important, most loved, and all her attention was on you. Lord, You were so gentle with her and the way I saw You love her opened my eyes to how You love me.

I got to experience an amazing memory of her a few weeks before she went. We were in the living room, I was playing guitar and singing a song You gave me for her called LU. She told me how special I was to You and that You love me so much. Megan was a gift from You who was too special for this world. She was too special to stay long.

She was like a shooting star who flashes in the sky for a brief moment just to give a glimpse of how beautiful the creation from the creator really is. I'm honored to have loved her the way I did and still do. I'm honored to have experienced the love she had for me and to spend half my life with my partner in life and best friend. I see her everywhere now, especially in Tony. Thank You so much for her, Lord. I live for the day to be reunited with her when we can fly like streamers in the wind of your endless atmosphere.

Every obstacle I face in this life, I don't battle directly. It is something you have already overcome.

A man can make his plans, but it is You, Lord, who guides our steps.

Adonai,

Let Your will be established on earth.

Adonai,

I love You. Your grace is sufficient. I trust You. Help me with my unbelief. Thank You for the way You love me. You know my heart. Help me to open up to You, Abba. You can see where I'm hurting, and there is healing in Your wings. I feel like the carpet has been pulled from underneath, and You're the only one who can get me back on my feet again.

You overwhelm me with grace. You shine. You eliminate evil. It is afraid of You and runs from You. Its intentions are revealed to the one who knows everything. Your love is felt by me, and it is warm and embracing. Your love reassures me that I have a loving God who did, does, and will do anything to keep me in his embrace. Nothing can separate me from Your love. Your love is strong.

Help me to see You from the inside. By faith not by sight. Help me to see the things that are far off, like the fathers of faith. Help me to see with my soul through Your spirit, to press my head against the magenta. To know that she has a dance saved for me and that You have a dance saved for the both of us. I love you, Angel. When I fall, You set me down gentle like snow, Lord. You burn in my bones. Where would I go away from You?

You have the words of eternal life. You are my eternal reward. Once I have seen, I now know. Now that I know, I will never be the same. From the burning bush, Moses's life was changed forever. On the road to Damascus, Saul's life was changed forever. From the night You called Samuel by name, his life was changed forever. You ignite the flame and forever a fire in our bones. There is no forgetting a meeting with the Creator. Changed for life.

Megan's TD Jakes notes January 19, 2018

    He's mine and nobody can take him, He's mine nobody can rob me of him, All together lovely, My kinsman redeemer, My joy, My strength, My peace, the meek and humble lamb, the Rose of Sharon, the lily in the valley, the bright and morning star, My turtledove, My trumpet, My peace, My fortress, My mighty God, El Shaddai, Jehovah Rohi, My savior, My King, My deliverer, My bridge over troubled water, My HEALING, My STRENGTH, My LIFE, My shield, My sword, My defender, My lawyer, My justice, My lover, My mother, My father, My sister, My brother, He is the lifter of my head, whatever you want, whatever you need, whatever you ask, whatever you seek, Jesus… demons tremble, hell gets nervous, sickness flees, dead men rise up, grave opener, <u>JESUS</u>

16

In Closing

Job 19:23 (NKJV)
"Oh, that my words were written! Oh, that they were inscribed in a book!"

How do I close or finish a book I never thought I would write? I would have never guessed that my first letter would have brought me to this point where I am contemplating the end of a book, a part of my own adventure with God, written in pages. I often wonder what would happen if I were able to go back in time and tell my twenty-two-year-old self that out of his confusion and brokenness, out of his search for truth and yearning to love and be loved, he would find a way of communicating with God by writing a letter.

That God would actually answer him back, lead him out of his town and into an adventure with the Creator of all things. That he would marry a woman beyond his dreams. That he would explore places like Japan, Australia, Hawaii, California, Thailand, China, Italy, and Singapore. That he would be a father to an amazing boy who will one day become a man himself and will have a chance to live out his own adventure with God.

My twenty-two-year-old self would tell me that I was crazy if I told him that the letters to God would not just stop at the first, but would become a multitude of letters. That the same method of communication with God would continue throughout his whole life. That all of the letters he had to God, letters written on loose leaf sheets, letters written on napkins, receipts, and in notebooks would all be compiled together along with the letters to Megan to fill a composite book. That those words would not just be letters in a composite book but would actually become Letters in Vessels, a real book.

That young man would never leave the house if I were to tell him that his dying wife would inspire him to take advantage of the time he had, to hang onto it, to experience it and take it in. I can remember typing this book into the computer and Megan asking me what I was writing. When I told her that it was this book, I could feel her cheering me on. I can feel her cheering me on now as I type away like a machine on a mission as a way to grieve her loss. I'm not sure who is going to read this when I am done. Maybe one of those readers will be that young man who I would like to go back in time to talk to.

Letters in Vessels was written in accident. I started the letters to talk to the Lord. It is by His grace that it became a book. I strongly believe that there were other men who probably felt the same way as I do today. Like David pouring his heart out in writing at the caves of Adullam. I am sure in the moment he did not realize that one day these eyes would read his same words. Or like Paul, while in the darkness of prisons, bleeding the ink on paper in his letters to the churches. I am sure that he was unaware that those letters would not only reach those churches but nations around the world. Or like Moses, in the midst of his own people believing that slavery was better than the Exodus. I am glad that in the center of diversity and doubt, Moses wrote down his exodus. If he did not, it would have never led to my own exodus. Even though those men have been dead for thousands of years, their communication with God and the people around them through the written word would bring life to all who believe. There is no time that could stop what they have written because the words that were written many years ago are the same as their creator: the beginning and the end.

> Revelation 14:13 (NKJV)
> "Then I heard a voice from heaven saying to me, 'Write: "Blessed are the dead who die in the Lord from now on."'"
> "Yes," says the Spirit, "that they may rest from their labors, and their works follow them."

If your eyes can see these words, I pray that you will also see God's deep love and compassion for you. Even though life can be messy, painful, sweet, and beautiful—somedays, all in the same time. Wherever we are in life, God will never change throughout it. He is steady in His love for us and wants us to have a deep relationship with Himself. All of the beautiful gifts He has put in each of us—whether it be talking, dancing, writing, making music, or building—He wants us to use these gifts as a way of communication and expression of our love toward Him, worship. He loves us and loves for us to love Him back. In this relationship, which is built on the bonds of love, an adventure will unfold.

> "I always believed that I have something important to say and I said it." ([10]Reed, "Lou Reed Quotes," Brainy Quotes. http://www.brainyquotes.com/quotes/lou_reed_25508)

Short Notes

[1] Linberg and Stevenson, Oxford American Dictionary, 1003.
[2] ALL, Alverez and Stevenson. "Until Then."
[3] STP and Weiland. "Still Remains."
[4] Benge, One Great Purpose, Synopsis.
[5] Tozer, The Knowledge of The Holy, 33.
[6] Lewis and Neeson. The Chronicles of Narnia/Prince Caspian. DVD.
[7] Bentman, "Man Was Made to Mourn." The Poetical Works of Burns. 36.
[8] Hendrix, Brainy Quotes. http://brainyquotes/Jimi_Hendrix_195397
[9] Doyle, Mieder and Shapiro, The Dictionary of Modern Proverbs, 239.
[10] Reed, "Lou Reed Quotes," Brainy Quotes. http://www.brainy-quotes.com/quotes/lou_reed_25508

Notes

[1] Christine A. Linberg and Angus Stevenson, Oxford American Dictionary Third Edition (New York: Oxford University Press Inc. 2010), 1003.
[2] ALL, Karl Alverez and Bill Stevenson. "Until Then." Mass Nerder, Colorado: The Blasting Room. Los Angeles: Epitaph Records, 1998.
[3] Stone Temple Pilots and Scott Weiland. "Still Remains." Purple, California: The Record Plant. New York City: Atlantic Records, 1994.

[4] Geoff and Janet Benge, One Great Purpose (Seattle WA: YWAM Pub., 1999), Synopsis.

[5] A.W. Tozer, The Knowledge of The Holy (New York City: Harper Collins Publishers, 1961), 33.

[6] Liam Neeson and C.S. Lewis. The Chronicles of Narnia: Prince Caspian. DVD. Directed by Andrew Adamson. Los Angeles: Walt Disney Pictures and Alden Media, 2008.

[7] Raymond Bentman, The Poetical Works of Burns (Boston: Houghton Mifflin Company, 1974), 36.

[8] Jimi Hendrix, "Jimi Hendrix- When the Power of Love," Brainy Quotes, Accessed September 14, 2019, http://www.brainyquotes/Jimi_Hendrix_195397

[9] Charles Clay Doyle, Wolfgang Mieder and Fred Shapiro, The Dictionary of Modern Proverbs (New Haven: Yale University Press, 2012), 239.

[10] Lou Reed, "Lou Reed Quotes" Brainy Quotes, Accessed September 14, 2019, https://www.brainyquotes.com/quotes/lou_reed_25508

Bibliography

ALL, Alverez, Karl and Stevenson, Bill. "Until Then." Mass Nerder, Colorado The Blasting Room. Los Angeles Epitaph Records, 1998.

Benge, Geoff and Janet. One Great Purpose. Seattle YWAM Pub, 1999. 185-Synopsis.

Bentman, Raymond and Burns, Robert. The Poetical Works of Burns. "Man Was Made to Mourn." Boston Houghton Mifflin Company, 1974. 30-40.

Doyle, Charles Clay, Mieder, Wolfgang and Shapiro, Fred. The Dictionary of Modern Proverbs. New Haven Yale University Press, 2012. 200-250.

Hendrix, Jimi, "Jimi Hendrix- When the Power of Love," Brain Quotes, Accessed September 14, 2019, http://www.brainyquotes/Jimi_Hendrix_195397

Linberg, Christin A. and Stevenson, Angus. Oxford American Edition Third Edition. New York Oxford University Press Inc, 2010. 1000-1010.

Neeson, Liam and Lewis, C.S. The Chronicles of Narnia/Prince Caspian. DVD. Directed by Andrew Adamson. Los Angeles Walt Disney Pictures and Walden Media, 2008.

Reed, Lou, "Lou Reed Quotes" Brainy Quotes, Accessed September 14, 2019, http://www.brainyquotes.com/quotes/lou_reed_25508

Stone Temple Pilots, Weiland, Scott. "Still Remains." Purple, Los Angeles The Record Plant. New York City Atlantic Records, 1994.

Letters in Vessels

Tozer, A.W. The Knowledge of The Holy. New York City Harper Collins Publishers, 1961. 30-35.

Letter 1 of 3

^A Matthew 23:12, ^B Ezekiel 37:21, ^C Proverbs 8:4, ^D Job 27:3 and Genesis 2:7, ^E Ezekiel 2:7, ^F Deuteronomy 26:1, ^G Zechariah 4:6, ^H Isaiah 45:2 and Deuteronomy 31:8, ^I 1Timothy 1:14, John 1:16 and 2Corinthians 12:9, ^J John 14:27, ^K Matthew 16:24 and John 15:7, ^L John 19:11 and Luke 10:19, ^M Deuteronomy 31:8, ^N Isaiah 40:29, ^O John 3:16, ^P Matthew 11:28, Exodus 33:14 and Isaiah 48:22, ^Q John 8:12 and 1John 1:5

Letter 2 of 3

^2A Proverbs 3:5, ^2B John 6:37 and Deuteronomy 31:16, ^2C Mark 11:22 and Genesis 1:1, ^2D Isaiah 55:9, ^2E Psalm 22:7, ^2F Genesis 1:1, ^2G Isaiah 59:3 and Leviticus 18:25, ^2H Deuteronomy 32:5 and Mark 9:19, ^2I Psalm 94:9, ^2J Acts 3:19, ^2K Matthew 11:29 and Proverbs 9:10, ^2L Romans 10:13, ^2M Jerimiah 32:27, ^2N Psalm 103:8, ^2O 1John 2:2, ^2P 1Peter 2:24, ^2Q Luke 9:23 and Psalm 30:5, ^2R Psalm 103:16 and 1Peter 1:4, ^2S Proverbs 3:5

Letter 3 of 3

^3A Psalm 139:3 and Psalm 139:15, ^3B 1Timothy 4:4, ^3C 2Corinthians 6:18, ^3D Matthew 11:28, ^3E Matthew 11:29, ^3F John 14:1, ^3G John 1:4, ^3H Psalm 139:2, ^3I Psalm 56:8, ^3J John 11:35, ^3K Numbers 6:25, ^3L 1John 3:1and 2 ^3M Matthew 22:37-39, ^3N Matthew 11:28 and Isaiah 41:10, ^3O Psalm 11:29 and Mark 16:15, ^3P Isaiah 9:7, ^3Q John 1:3, ^3R Galatians 1:4, ^3S 1Peter 2:24, ^3T John 3:16, ^3U Jeremiah 2:13, ^3V Matthew 4:19 and John 14:6, ^3W John 14:27 and John 10:10, ^3X John 16:33 ^3Y Isaiah 9:6, ^3Z Mark 8:36, ^3A3 Jeremiah 29:11, ^3B3 1Peter 4:10, ^3C3 Romans 8:28,

Bibliography

[3D3] Jeremiah 29:13 and Proverbs 8:17, [3E3] Matthew 7:7, [3F3] Romans 5:8, [3G3] Isaiah 41:10, [3H3] Psalm 39:3, [3I3] Psalm 118:14, [3J3] Jeremiah 17:14 and Exodus 14:30, [3K3] Matthew 6:6, [3L3] John 13:34, Isaiah 55:11 and Hebrews 4:12, [3M3] John 6:63, [3N3] Psalm 119:105, [3O3] Jeremiah 29:11-14, [3P3] Isaiah 43:1, [3Q3] Joshua 1:5, [3R3] Psalm 27:10, [3S3] Numbers 23:19, [3T3] Psalm 94:14, [3U3] Matthew 13:46, [3V3] 1John 3:16, [3W3] Mark 12:30, [3X3] Mark 12:31

CPSIA information can be obtained
at www.ICGtesting.com
Printed in the USA
FFHW011126301119
56533649-62325FF

9 781630 501365